Law Esser

D0274061

DELICT

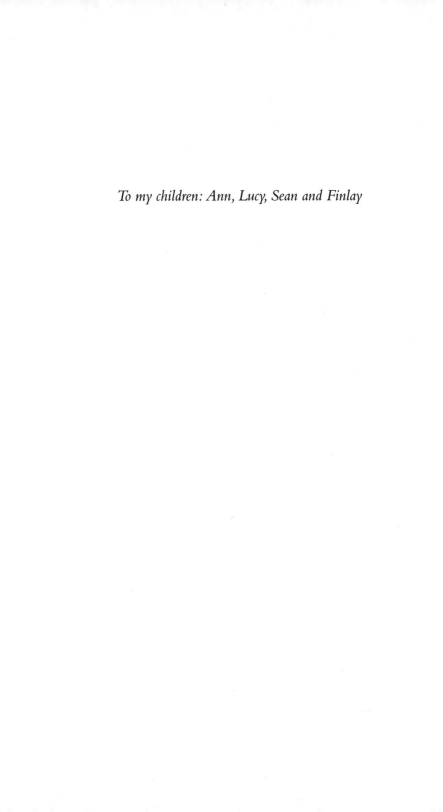

To my children: Ann, Lucy, Sean and Finlay

Law Essentials

DELICT

Francis McManus, M.Litt., LL.B.(Hons),
F.R.I.P.H., F.H.E.A., M.R.E.H.I.S., Cert. Ed.

Professor of Law, Napier University

DUNDEE UNIVERSITY PRESS
2008

First published in Great Britain in 2008 by
Dundee University Press
University of Dundee
Dundee DD1 4HN

www.dundee.ac.uk/dup

ISBN 1–84586–034–9

No natural forests were destroyed to make this product;
only farmed timber was used and replanted.

British Library Cataloguing-in-Publication Data
A catalogue for this book is available on request from the British Library.

Typeset by Waverley Typesetters, Fakenham
Printed and bound by Bell & Bain Ltd, Glasgow

CONTENTS

TABLE OF CASES

TABLE OF STATUTES

1 INTRODUCTION

The law of delict is concerned with civil wrongs, that is to say the law which governs compensation or reparation for damage which one individual inflicts upon another. The law imposes upon the person who injures another an obligation to compensate that person. The obligation which is thus imposed arises *ex lege* (by law), in contrast to that which arises *ex contractu* (by way of contract).

The law imposes a unilateral obligation on the person who commits a wrongful act to compensate the person who is injured. Such injury or harm may take a number of forms. It may take the form of injury which is caused to one's person, for example that caused by a road accident or an accident at work. However, the injury or damage which is the subject-matter of an action in delict may take quite different forms. I might sustain financial loss because I have relied on negligent advice which was given to me by my financial adviser who suggested that I should invest money in a newly floated company which soon goes into liquidation. The harm in question may take more subtle forms. For example, it could consist of the loss of my reputation or of hurt feelings as a result of what has been written about me. The law of defamation allows me to recover for such injury in certain circumstances. Again, the injury could comprise my being annoyed by my neighbour's constant guitar playing. The law of nuisance can provide a remedy in such circumstances.

However, not every human act which causes injury or harm allows one to be compensated in the law of delict. For example, a petrol station may be put out of business soon after a large supermarket petrol station commences operation in the vicinity. The proprietor of the former would have no remedy in the law of delict since, in the eye of the law, the owners of the supermarket have done no wrong.

There are a number of theories on the function and role of the law of delict. The respective theories overlap. Occasionally, judges refer to such theories in their judgments. However, in the majority of cases they do not.

Some argue that the law of delict operates to control the behaviour of people before they perform a particular act which has the potential to cause harm. I, therefore, refrain from consuming alcohol before I set out on a car journey because I know that if I injure a fellow road user I could be sued. I refrain from assaulting you for the same reason. However, one could argue that in such cases it is not the fear that I may be required to compensate my victim that prompts me to act in a non-delictual way, but, rather, fear of my incurring sanction under the criminal law: I might be sent to jail for drunk-driving or assaulting you! One could also argue that another reason for my refraining from acting in a delictual way is not fear of any form of legal sanction, whether civil or criminal, but rather fear of public opprobrium. The public, generally speaking, think less of people who act in such a manner.

Another function of the law of delict is based on distributive justice. This principle is founded on the premise that by spreading the loss from an individual victim to those who benefit from an activity, the loss is more easily borne in terms of society as a whole. For example, a public utility which is forced to compensate someone who is injured in a gas explosion is able to absorb the cost by raising the price of its service among those who benefit from it, namely the public. Another example of the principle of distributive justice is seen in the concept of vicarious liability. Here, an employer (who can more easily bear the legal obligation to compensate the victim than his employee) is held strictly liable (that is to say, liable without fault) for the delicts of his employees. The same principle applies to a situation in which a defective product injures a consumer. The producer can spread his loss (represented in terms of his obligation to compensate the victim) by raising the price of his products.

However, some are of the view that the requirements of distributive justice can also be satisfied simply by allowing the loss to lie where it falls. For example, in *McFarlane* v *Tayside Health Board* (2000) the pursuers were negligently advised that a vasectomy had rendered the husband infertile. The couple relied on that advice and ceased to take contraceptive precautions. A child was born to them. The couple sued the health board for the financial loss which they would incur in bringing up the child. However, the House of Lords rejected their claim. Lord Steyn was of the view (at 82) that such losses were those which society (some of whom wanted but could not have children, others who had to bring up disabled children) as a whole had to bear. It would not be morally acceptable for the law to transfer to the health board the loss in respect of which the pursuer claimed compensation.

The main function of the law of delict is to compensate the victim for the damage or injury which he has sustained, whether such damage sounds in terms of economic loss or physical injury. Again, the injury for which the pursuer seeks compensation may take less obvious forms. This would, for example, be the case were I to seek compensation from the courts for the sleepless nights which I have endured as a result of the all-night parties which my next-door neighbour has been having for the past several months.

The law of delict, unlike, for example, the law of evidence or the law of succession, consists of a number of separate delicts. Indeed, there is no logical reason why this book could not have been entitled *Delicts*. Some delicts, such as assault, comprise intentional acts on the part of the defender, whereas other delicts, such as negligence, do not. Furthermore, in some delicts, such as nuisance and defamation, there also exist elements of intention and negligence. For example, I may intend to publish a defamatory statement about a particular person but not about the defender of whose existence I should have known.

There are thus a variety of delicts which are recognised by law. This book simply covers those which are considered to be the more important.

2 NEGLIGENCE

The vast majority of civil actions which are brought before the courts are negligence actions. Negligent conduct can take many forms. It can consist of accidents which occur at work by virtue of an employer's negligence. The negligent conduct could also comprise negligent driving on the roads or the giving of negligent advice by a financial adviser to a client.

What we must examine is how the courts have attempted to ascertain whether liability exists for harm which is caused by various forms of negligent conduct. We will see that, for policy reasons, the courts are more willing to allow a negligence claim to succeed for certain types of injury than for others.

In order to recover for damage which is caused by negligent conduct, the pursuer requires to prove that:

(1) the defender owes the pursuer a *duty of care* in law;

(2) the *standard of care* which the law demands of the defender has been breached; and

(3) the negligent act in question *caused* the requisite injury to the pursuer.

(1) DUTY OF CARE

In order to ascertain whether the defender is liable in law for the damage which he has caused, the court must decide whether the defender owed the pursuer a duty of care in law.

During the 19th century, with the advent of road and rail transport and, indeed, industrialisation in general, negligence actions were increasingly being brought before the courts. By the end of the century the courts had already established that a doctor owed a duty of care to a patient in respect of the treatment which was given to the patient; a road user owed a duty of care to another in respect of the former's conduct on the road; and an occupier of land, in certain circumstances, owed a duty of care to those who visited the land. However, the courts had never really worked out a general formula whereby one could establish whether the defender owed a duty of care to the pursuer in a novel situation, that is to say a situation or circumstances which had not previously been decided by the courts.

There had been several attempts by judges to work out such a formula. However, the real breakthrough came with the landmark decision of the House of Lords in *Donoghue* v *Stevenson* (1932). In that case Mrs Donoghue went into a café in Paisley. Her friend brought her an ice cream and a ginger beer. The ginger beer had been manufactured by Stevenson. The café proprietor poured some of the ginger beer into Mrs Donoghue's glass and she consumed some of the contents. Her friend then poured the remainder of the ginger beer into her glass. As he did so, the remains of a decomposed snail floated out of the bottle. Mrs Donoghue claimed that she suffered nervous shock and gastro-enteritis as a consequence. Of course, Mrs Donoghue did not have a contract with Stevenson, since her friend had bought the ginger beer from the café proprietor. Therefore, in order to succeed, she had to sue Stevenson in the law of delict. The question which the court had to answer was whether the manufacturer of the beer, Stevenson, owed a duty of care to Mrs Donoghue as the consumer. The House of Lords held that a duty of care was owed by the former to the latter. Lord Atkin stated:

> "The rule that you are to love your neighbour becomes in law, you must not injure your neighbour ... You must take reasonable care to avoid acts or omissions which would be likely to injure your neighbour. Who then is my neighbour? ... persons who are so closely affected by my act that I ought reasonably to have them in contemplation as being so affected when I am directing my mind to the acts or omissions which are called into question."

In other words, according to Lord Atkin, if one could reasonably foresee that one's conduct could harm the pursuer, a duty of care would arise.

A good example of the Atkinian foreseeability can be seen in *Beaumont* v *Surrey County Council* (1968). Here, a teacher discarded a long piece of elastic in an open bin. The elastic was used in horseplay between pupils and the plaintiff lost an eye. The education authority was held liable since it was foreseeable that such an accident would take place. The foreseeability principle was applied again in the House of Lords case of *Home Office* v *Dorset Yacht Company* (1970). In that case a party of Borstal trainees were working on Brownsea Island in Poole Harbour, under the supervision and control of three Borstal officers. During the night, seven of the trainees escaped and went aboard a yacht which was anchored nearby. The boys could not navigate properly, which resulted in a collision and damage to a yacht owned by the Dorset Yacht Company which successfully sued the Home Office in negligence. Essentially, the House of Lords held that the defendant owed a duty of care to the plaintiffs because such an occurrence was foreseeable. Lord Reid stated: "the time has come when we can and should say that (Lord Atkin's neighbour principle) ought to apply unless there is some justification or valid explanation for excluding liability in negligence".

It can be seen that Lord Reid is suggesting that a duty of care should be held to exist if one can foresee that one's conduct will injure someone else. However, that duty of care would be negated if policy reasons dictated.

Two-staged approach

Lord Reid's approach really implied that one should take a two-staged approach in ascertaining whether a duty of care should lie between the defender and the pursuer. The scene was, therefore, set for the for the formal endorsement of such an approach in the House of Lords case of *Anns* v *Merton London Borough Council* (1977). In that case a builder negligently constructed the foundations of a building which was being constructed and the walls began to crack. The owner of the building sued the local authority (which was responsible for ensuring that the building works complied with the relevant building control legislation), in effect, for failing to protect him from incompetent builders. The House of Lords held that the local authority did owe the owner a duty of care in law. Lord Wilberforce enunciated a two-staged approach to the duty of care. In his view, if the court were confronted with a novel situation (that is to say, one which had not come before the courts previously) one should approach the concept of duty of care in the following way:

(a) first, if a sufficient relationship of proximity exists between the parties then, *prima facie*, a duty of care arises; and

(b) second, if such a duty of care does arise, it is then necessary to consider whether there are any considerations which ought to negative, reduce or limit the scope of such duty.

In deciding if there was a sufficiently close relationship, one would still rely on the foreseeability test of Lord Atkin in *Donoghue* v *Stevenson* (1932). However, if one formed the view that a duty of care arose, one would ascertain if there were any policy grounds for excluding liability. We can see here that such an approach to the duty of care allows a court to extend the boundaries of the law of negligence fairly readily. A good example of the courts using the two-staged approach to expand the duty of care is seen in *McLoughlin* v *O'Brian* (1983). In that case the House of Lords had to consider whether a mother who sustained nervous shock by visiting, in hospital, her family who had been seriously injured by the negligence of the defendant could succeed in a negligence action. Prior to the case being decided it was necessary that a secondary victim of nervous shock had to witness the actual accident itself before he could succeed in a negligence claim. However, the House used the two-staged approach to the duty of care to allow her to recover.

However, this expansive approach to the duty of care was relatively short lived. In *Governors of the Peabody Fund* v *Sir Lindsay Parkinson* (1985) the House of Lords had to consider whether a local authority was liable to building contractors for failing to ascertain at the time of inspection that the drains which were being installed on a building site were unsuitable. In holding that the local authority was not liable for the loss which was sustained the House took into account not only whether there was sufficient proximity between the defendant and the plaintiff but also whether it would be fair, just and reasonable to impose a duty of care. Several years later, in *Yuen Kun-Yeu* v *Attorney-General of Hong Kong* (1987), individuals who had deposited money in a bank sued the Government, in effect, for failing to regulate a bank properly, resulting in their losing money. The Privy Council was of the view that the law should develop novel categories of negligence incrementally and by analogy rather than by a massive extension of a *prima facie* duty of care which was restrained only by indefinable considerations which sought to negative, reduce or limit the scope of the duty or class of person to whom it is owed. In other words, the Privy Council advocated an approach in which more sanctity would be accorded to previously decided cases. If a novel factual set of circumstances were presented before the court it would ascertain whether the courts had decided a case which was analogous to the present facts. In any case, the law should allow the boundaries of the duty of care to be expanded gradually or incrementally.

Another decisive blow against the two-staged approach to the duty of care came with the decision in *Caparo* v *Dickman* (1990). In that case shareholders brought an action in negligence against auditors, on the ground that the latter had negligently prepared an audit, the consequences of which were that the shareholders had purchased shares in reliance on the relevant report and had suffered financial loss. The House of Lords held that no duty of care was owed by the auditors to the shareholders. A relationship of proximity or neighbourhood was required to exist between the plaintiffs and the defendants. The House also had to consider it fair, just and reasonable that the law should impose a duty of a given scope. Furthermore, foreseeability and proximity were different things. Foreseeability was a necessary but not a sufficient requirement to establish a duty of care in negligence.

The current incremental approach to the duty of care is well illustrated in *Hill* v *Chief Constable of West Yorkshire* (1989) in which the mother of one of the victims of the "Yorkshire Ripper" (Peter Sutcliffe) sued the Chief Constable for failure to apprehend the Ripper. It was held that no duty of care was owed by the defendant, even though it was reasonably foreseeable that if Sutcliffe was not apprehended, he would inflict serious injury on members of the public. Lord Keith was of the view that it was against public policy to hold the police civilly liable for failure to apprehend a criminal. He stated:

> "A great deal of time, trouble and expense might be expected to have to be put into the preparation of the defence to the action and attendance of witnesses at the trial. The result would be a significant diversion of police manpower and attention from their most important function, that of suppression of crime"(at 63).

Again, in *X* v *Bedfordshire County Council* (1995) the House of Lords essentially had to decide whether or not to impose a common law duty of care in negligence in respect of a local authority failing to take appropriate measures to protect the plaintiffs against child abuse. The House refused to do so, on the basis that that would discourage the due performance of the local authority's statutory duties. However, in *Barrett* v *Enfield London Borough Council* (2001) the claimant had been placed in the care of the defendant local authority when he was 10 months old and remained there until he was 17. He claimed that the authority had been under a duty to show him the standard of care which would be expected of a responsible parent to protect him from physical and emotional injury etc. The House of Lords held that the public policy considerations which meant that it would not be fair, just and reasonable to impose a common law duty of care did not have the same force in respect of decisions taken after the claimant had been taken into care. Another reason why the House was willing to accept that a duty of care could lie in law was that once the child was actually in the care of the local authority, it was easier to ascertain whether the defendant had breached the standard of care which the law imposed on it. It was, therefore, easier to impose a duty of care on the defendant.

However, English cases such as *X* v *Bedfordshire County Council* (1995), where the courts were unwilling to impose liability in negligence for so-called "pure omissions" of public bodies, may not represent the law of Scotland and therefore should be treated with caution. In the Outer House case of *Burnett* v *Grampian Fire and Rescue Services* (2007) (which concerned liability on the part of a fire brigade for failure to extinguish a fire which damaged the pursuer's premises) Lord Macphail stated *obiter* that the law of Scotland does not draw a distinction between acts and omissions, as far as the law of negligence is concerned.

An important question which fell to be answered in the wake of the incremental approach being instituted was whether, in determining whether a duty of care existed, one should adopt a similar approach to claims which pertain to physical harm as to those pertaining to economic loss. In *Marc Rich and Co* v *Bishop Rock Marine Ltd* (1996) a ship was negligently surveyed by the defendant. It was put to sea in reliance on the survey. However, the ship was damaged and soon sank, resulting in its loss and also that of the cargo. It was held that the law should not draw any distinction between the type of harm which the plaintiff sustains when ascertaining whether a duty of care lies. In other words, the incremental approach was appropriate irrespective of the type of loss which was sustained.

Another interesting example of the incremental approach to the duty of care can be seen in *Watson* v *British Boxing Board of Control* (2001). This case concerned head injuries sustained by Michael Watson, a professional boxer, in his title fight with Chris Eubank. The fight was regulated by the British Boxing Board of Control (BBBC). Watson claimed that the BBBC had failed to take adequate measures to ensure that he received immediate and effective medical attention should he sustain injury during the fight. The Court of Appeal held that there was sufficient proximity between the parties to ground a duty of care in law. Since the BBBC had complete control over the contest it was fair, just and reasonable to conclude that a duty of care existed. In his judgment (at 1281) Lord Phillips set store by the following factors:

(1) Watson was one of a defined number of boxing members of the BBBC.

(2) A primary stated object of the BBBC was to look after its boxing members' physical safety.

(3) The BBBC encouraged and supported its boxing members in the pursuit of an activity which involved inevitable physical injury.

(4) The BBBC controlled the medical assistance which could be provided.

(5) The BBBC had access to specialist expertise in relation to medical care.

(6) If Watson had no remedy against the BBBC, he had no remedy at all.

(7) Boxing members of the BBBC, including Watson, could reasonably rely on the former to look after their safety.

Factor 1 neatly illustrates the disinclination of the courts to impose on a defender a duty of care to a potentially large number of people. We will see this approach illustrated again in relation to claims for pure economic loss, loss sustained because of negligent statements and psychiatric injury.

The factual duty of care

What we have looked at so far is really the notional or nominal duty of care. That is to say, the court assesses a novel situation and determines whether it can, in law, impose a duty of care on the defender. However, once the court has decided that such a duty exists it must then proceed to ascertain, *on the facts of the case,* whether the defender owes the pursuer a duty of care by posing a risk of injury to the pursuer. This point can be neatly illustrated by two leading cases. The first is American.

In *Palsgraf* v *Long Island Railroad Co* (1928), a passenger was running to catch one of the defendant's trains. The defendant's servants, trying to assist the passenger to board it, dislodged a package from the passenger's arms and it fell upon the rails. The package contained fireworks which exploded with some violence. The explosion overturned some scales many metres away on the platform. The scales fell upon the plaintiff and injured her. The defendant's servants could not have foreseen that their act of negligence could have had such consequences to the plaintiff. Judge Cardozo, speaking for the majority of the court, held that there was no liability because there was no negligence to the plaintiff. In his view, negligence was required to be founded upon the relation between the parties which must be founded upon the foreseeability of harm to the person who was actually injured, not someone else.

The Scottish equivalent of *Palsgraf* is the leading case of *Bourhill* v *Young* (1942). There, a pregnant fishwife had just alighted from a tram when she heard the sound of a road accident. The accident had been caused by the negligence of a motorcyclist, John Young, who was overtaking the tram in which Mrs Bourhill had been travelling. Young collided with a car which was turning right and into his direction of travel. Mrs Bourhill did not see the accident taking place but, nevertheless, she suffered nervous shock. The House of Lords held that, whereas motorists and cyclists who use the roads owe a duty of care to fellow road users and pedestrians, on the facts of the case the defender did not owe the pursuer a duty of care. The former could not reasonably foresee that someone where Mrs Bourhill was situated when the accident took place would have sustained nervous shock.

Conclusions on the duty of care: the general part

What we have been covering thus far can best be described as the "general part" of the duty of care. However, there are certain discrete areas where the courts have had to refine the rules which we have looked at, for a number of reasons, often to reduce the number of claims which can be made. These will now be considered.

Pure economic loss

The general rule is that there is no liability for causing pure economic loss, that is to say loss which is not prefaced on physical injury to the pursuer. For example, if I am injured at work by a defective machine as a result of which I lose the opportunity to do overtime, the loss which I sustain would certainly fall to be described as "economic loss" but not "*pure* economic loss" since the loss derives from physical harm. However, if the local authority archives at which a historian is working are destroyed by a fire which has been negligently started by a clerk who is employed there, the upshot of which is that the historian cannot complete a book which he is in the course of writing and he loses royalty payments from his potential publisher, the loss to the historian would rank as pure economic loss since none of the historian's property has been damaged. He could not, therefore, recover for his lost royalties.

The rule that the law sets its face against allowing the pursuer to recover for pure economic loss is well illustrated in *Spartan Steel and Alloys Ltd* v *Martin and Co (Contractors) Ltd* (1972). In this case the claimants operated a steel factory. The factory obtained electricity by direct cable from a power station. Martin and Co were building contractors. The company used power-driven tools to carry out excavating work. In the course of carrying out such work a shovel fractured a cable and the electricity supply to the factory was shut off, causing a "melt" to be damaged. It was also established that during the time when the electricity supply was unavailable the claimant could have put more melts through the furnace. The plaintiffs brought an action against Martin in order to recover all damages which had been incurred. However, the Court of Appeal held that the plaintiffs were only entitled to recover for the loss to the particular melt and not for the economic loss or loss of revenue or productivity which was represented by a loss of other melts which might have been put through the furnace had the power supply not failed. According to Lord Denning MR (at 38):

> "if claims for pure economic loss were permitted for this particular hazard there would be no end of claims. Some might be genuine but many might

be inflated or even false. A machine might not have been in use anyway, but it would be easy to put it down to the cut in supply. It would be well-nigh impossible to check the claims."

Another case which illustrates the same principle is *Murphy* v *Brentwood District Council* (1990). In that case a local authority carried out its building inspection duties negligently because its building inspectors had failed to notice that a building had been erected on foundations which were of inadequate depth. The upshot of this was that the building's walls began to crack. The plaintiff sustained financial loss since the house could only be sold at a reduced price. The House of Lords held that since the relevant damage comprised solely injury to the premises themselves, such injury simply ranked as pure economic loss and was, therefore, irrecoverable. In the last analysis, the loss which the plaintiff had sustained was analogous to Messrs Stevenson, in the case of *Donoghue* v *Stevenson* (1932), negligently pouring undrinkable but, at the same time, harmless, ginger beer into a bottle and Mrs Donoghue, on discovering this, simply discarding the liquid before consuming any of it.

A more recent illustration of the reluctance of the courts to allow claims for pure economic loss is *McFarlane* v *Tayside Health Board* (2000). In that case the pursuers were negligently advised that a vasectomy had rendered the husband infertile. The couple relied on that advice and ceased to take contraceptive precautions. A child was born to them. The couple sued the health board for the financial loss which they would incur in bringing up the child. The House of Lords rejected their claim since such loss ranked as pure economic loss.

Negligent statements

In the leading case on liability for negligent statements, *Hedley Byrne* v *Heller* (1964), Lord Pearce stated: "words are more volatile than deeds. They travel fast and far afield. They are used without being expended". In effect, the potential number of people who could be affected by relying on a negligent statement is limitless. An advert which contains negligent advice (for example, that one should invest in certain companies which are in fact unsound) and which is placed in a popular newspaper could be read and relied on by hundreds of thousands of people. Such an advert which is placed on the Internet could be read by millions of people who could sustain financial loss. It is certainly foreseeable that a very large number of people could suffer financial harm in such circumstances. However, the question of liability for unlimited sums of money to an unlimited class of individuals is something that the courts are unwilling to countenance. Therefore, in effect, the courts have had to introduce certain checks in order to cut down the potential number of claimants.

The leading case on the subject of harm caused by negligent statements is *Hedley Byrne* v *Heller* (1964). There, Easypower, a firm, asked Hedley Byrne to do some work for it. In order to ascertain whether Easypower could afford to pay the claimant, it asked its bank (National Provincial) to enquire of Easypower's bank (Heller), whether Easypower could afford the services of Hedley Byrne. Heller informed Hedley Byrne that Easypower was financially sound but, at the same time, expressly disclaimed liability for the accuracy of the information it gave. Easypower was not, in fact, financially sound and Hedley Byrne lost money. Hedley Byrne therefore sued Heller and the House of Lords held that in the absence of a disclaimer the defendant would have been liable. However, the judges differed in their approaches as to when one should hold that a duty of care was owed by someone who had made a negligent statement. According to Lord Morris (at 502 and 503), a duty of care would arise if someone possessed of special skill undertakes, quite irrespective of a contract, to apply that skill. However, Lord Devlin was of the view that in order for a duty of care to arise the relationship between the maker of the negligent statement and the recipient must be equivalent to that existing under a contract. That is to say that the relationship must be close. The House was generally of the view that there must be some assumption of responsibility on the part of the maker of the statement and also reliance on the part of the recipient. In the previously mentioned case of *Caparo* v *Dickman* (1990) Lord Oliver was of the view that in order to be liable for the making of a negligent statement the necessary relationship between the defender and the pursuer required to have four features:

(1) the advice is required for a purpose which is either specific or generally described which is made known to the adviser at the time the advice is given;

(2) the defender knows that the advice will be communicated to the advisee either individually or as a member of an ascertained class in order that it should be used by the advisee for that purpose;

(3) the defender knows that the advice is likely to be acted upon without independent enquiry; and

(4) the pursuer acts on the advice.

It is not sufficient that the defender knows that his advice will be relied on: *Galoo Ltd* v *Bright Graham Murray* (1994). Generally speaking, there will be no liability for statements which are made on a purely social occasion, since the maker of the statement implicitly accepts no responsibility for the statement: *Chaudhry* v *Prabhakar* (1989). It is also critical that the defender knows that the pursuer will be likely to rely on the statement without obtaining independent advice: *Smith* v *Eric S Bush Ltd* (1989). Moreover, it is not essential that the person to whom the statement is made solely relies on the statement and thereby incurs a loss: *JEB Fasteners Ltd* v *Marks Bloom and Co* (1983). Finally, it is not necessary that the statement be made directly to the person who sustains the loss in question. That is to say, the statement can be made to a third party who relies on the statement and acts on it to the detriment of the pursuer: *Spring* v *Guardian Assurance* (1994).

Psychiatric injury (nervous shock)

According to Professor Fleming in *The Law of Torts* (9th edn, 1998, p 73) if the law were to treat nervous shock in the same way as external injuries from physical impact, this would open up a wide field of imaginary claims. The law must, therefore, impose arbitrary limitations before it can extend the duty of care to embrace nervous shock. Such limitations can include the requirement that the shock must have resulted from the fear of injury to oneself or, at least, to one's near relative or one's witnessing an accident with one's own unaided senses, in order to reduce the potential number of pursuers. As with the case for liability for negligent statements, foreseeability of injury is by itself incapable of providing a solution as to whether the pursuer should recover.

It is usual for the courts to divide victims of nervous shock into primary victims and secondary victims. As a general rule, the courts will normally allow one to recover in respect of psychiatric injury only if one has been subjected to a traumatic event such as a road or an industrial accident. The only exception to this is that, in certain circumstances, one can recover in relation to psychiatric injury which is caused by stress at work: see, for example, *Fraser v State Hospitals Board for Scotland* (2001).

Primary victims

In order that one can recover as a primary victim of nervous shock, one must physically participate or be actively involved in the very events which cause the psychiatric injury: *Salter* v *UB Frozen and Chilled Foods Ltd* (2003). In the case of *Dooley* v *Cammell Laird Ltd* (1951) the claimant was operating a crane which was being used to unload a ship. The crane rope snapped and the load which was being carried plummeted into the hold of the ship where the plaintiff's colleagues were working. He sustained nervous shock as a result and successfully sued his employers.

The leading case on the subject of primary victims of nervous shock is now *Page* v *Smith* (1996). In this case the claimant, who was suffering from a condition known as chronic fatigue syndrome, was involved in a minor road accident. He was uninjured but his condition became permanent as a result of the accident. He successfully claimed damages in respect of this. The House of Lords refused to draw a distinction between psychiatric injury and physical injury. Essentially, the House of Lords held that notwithstanding the fact that the type of injury which the claimant sustained was not reasonably foreseeable, given the fact that physical injury to the claimant's person was, indeed, foreseeable, the law should not draw a distinction between these forms of injury as far as liability in negligence was concerned. It sufficed simply that some form of physical injury was foreseeable.

Secondary victims

The vast majority of claims relating to nervous shock concern secondary victims, that is to say those who have witnessed a traumatic and sustained harm as a consequence.

The leading case on this subject is now *Alcock* v *Chief Constable of South Yorkshire* (1991). There, the defendant was responsible for policing a football match. Overcrowding in part of the stadium was caused by the negligence of the police: 95 people were crushed to death. Many more people were seriously injured. Live pictures of the harrowing event were broadcast on television. The claimants were either all related to or were friends of the spectators who were involved in the disaster. Some people witnessed the traumatic events from other parts of the stadium. Others saw the events on television. However, all claimants alleged that they had suffered nervous shock. The House of Lords held that in order to succeed it was necessary for the claimants to show that the injury sustained was reasonably foreseeable and also that the relationship between the claimant and the defendant was sufficiently proximate. As far as the latter was concerned, the relationship between the claimants and the victims had to be one of both love and affection. Such a degree of affection would be assumed in certain cases, such as between parent and child or husband and wife. In other cases, however, the requisite affection would require to be proved. This would be the case in respect of remoter relationships such as cousins. Furthermore, the House of Lords held that the claimant was required to show propinquity (or closeness) in terms of time and space to the accident or its immediate aftermath. A fairly recent Scottish case in which *Alcock* was followed was *Keen* v *Tayside Contracts* (2003). In that case the pursuer, a road worker, had been instructed by his supervisor to attend the scene of a road accident. The pursuer witnessed badly crushed and burned bodies. He suffered psychiatric injury as a consequence. He sued his employers, in essence, for having exposed him to such traumatic circumstances. He failed in his action, on the basis that his injury was simply caused by him witnessing the traumatic event. In other words, he ranked in the eye of the law as a secondary victim. He was not related to any of the victims. Therefore, his action failed.

The duty of care and affirmative action

To what extent, if any, does the law impose a duty of care on the defender for simply failing to take appropriate action in respect of someone who is in need of help? The general rule is that the law refrains from imposing an affirmative duty on the defender. However, there are certain situations where the law does impose a duty on the defender to take affirmative action. The law imposes a duty of care on the defender not to allow his property to become a known source of danger to neighbouring proprietors: *Sedleigh-Denfield* v *O'Callaghan* (1940); *Goldman* v *Hargrave* (1967); and *Leakey* v *National Trust* (1980). The law will also require a person who stands in a particular relationship with the pursuer to protect him from harm: *Watson* v *British Boxing Board of Control* (2001). The relationships of parent–child, employer–employee, occupier of land–visitor and school–pupil have all attracted a duty of care on the person who exercised the relevant control. See also *Rice* v *Secretary of State for Trade and Industry* (2007).

Again, if, through my conduct, I encourage the pursuer to rely on me and then I negligently conduct a rescue, I am liable to the pursuer: *Christchurch Drainage Board* v *Brown* (1987). Sometimes the assumption of responsibility alone on the part of the defender towards the pursuer grounds liability for pure omissions: *White* v *Jones* (1995).

The defender may come under a duty to take affirmative action if he creates a risk: *Mooney* v *Lanark County Council* (1954).

Finally, there is some Commonwealth authority to the effect that if the defender derives some economic advantage from his relationship with the pursuer, the former owes a duty of care to the latter: *Crocker* v *Sundance Northwest Resorts Ltd* (1988).

(2) STANDARD OF CARE

Once it has been established that the defender owes a duty of care to the pursuer it is necessary to ascertain whether that duty of care has been breached. Whether the defender has failed to attain the standard of care which the law demands of him is judged objectively: that is to say, no account is taken of individual disabilities or idiosyncrasies, with the exception of children who are judged in terms of the standard of children of the age of the defender. The leading case on this point is *Nettleship* v *Weston* (1971). In that case a learner driver was held to be required to attain the same standard of driving as an ordinary competent driver.

The courts take into account a number of factors in order to decide whether the defender has been negligent. These are now discussed.

The state of current knowledge

The leading case relating to the state of current knowledge is *Roe* v *Minister of Health* (1954). In that case the plaintiff went into hospital for a minor operation. He was given a spinal injection. The fluid which was used for the injection was kept in an ampoule (a very small glass container) which in turn was kept in a phenol solution. However, at this time it was not known that phenol could seep into the ampoule, through invisible cracks. The plaintiff was paralysed from the waist downwards. He sued the Minister of Health who was responsible for the hospital concerned. His action failed because the defendant's hospital had not breached its standard of care since it had acted in a way in which any other reasonable hospital would have acted in the situation.

The magnitude of risk

The greater the risk of injury from the activity which is the subject-matter of the action, the greater the amount of precautions the defender is required to take. In *Blyth* v *Birmingham Waterworks Co* (1856) the defendant water board laid a water main which was 18 inches in depth. One year there was an extremely severe frost which penetrated the ground as far as the water main. The main burst and flooded the plaintiff's premises. It was held that the water board was not not negligent because it had taken reasonable precautions in the circumstances. A more recent case which illustrates the same point is *Bolton* v *Stone* (1951). In that case the plaintiff, while standing on a quiet suburban highway outside her home, was struck by a cricket ball. The plaintiff was situated 100 yards from the batsman and the ball had cleared a 17-foot fence which was situated 78 yards from him. Similar hits had occurred only about six times in the previous 30 years. The House of Lords held that since the likelihood of injury was small, the plaintiff had not established that the defendant had breached his duty of care towards the claimant.

The risk of serious harm

In determining whether the standard of care which the law demands of the defender has not been attained, one takes into account not simply the likelihood that the accident will occur but, rather, the seriousness of the injury should an accident occur. The leading case is *Paris v Stepney Borough Council* (1950). There, a one-eyed worker was injured while at work. He claimed that his employers should have provided and also required him to use goggles while he was working. It was proved that there was no greater likelihood that an accident would befall the plaintiff than a worker with normal sight. However, the House of Lords held that since the consequences of an injury to the plaintiff were graver, extra precautions were necessary.

The utility of the defender's activity

The social utility, or usefulness, of the relevant activity which is the subject-matter of the action is taken into account. The greater the utility, the less likely it is that the court will hold that the relevant standard of care has been breached. The leading case is *Watt v Hertfordshire County Council* (1954). The plaintiff was a fireman. One day his station received a call that a woman was trapped under a heavy lorry as a result of a road accident. A jack was required to lift the vehicle. Two of the plaintiff's colleagues threw a heavy jack on to a lorry in which they were to travel. However, the lorry was not designed to carry a jack. During the journey the jack rolled away from its original position and injured the plaintiff. It was held that the defendants had not been negligent. In reaching its decision the court took into account the social utility of the journey, namely the rescuing of an injured person. However, simply because the defender is involved in an activity which has some social worth does not automatically exonerate him from the need to take care. This point was decided in *Ward v London County Council* (1938). There, the driver of a fire engine was held to have been negligent in driving though a red traffic light and injuring the plaintiff. It was held that the defendant could not use the reason that he was involved in a journey of social worth as an excuse for his breach of duty of care.

The practicality of precautions

The easier it is to take measures to counteract the risk, the more likely it is that the courts will hold that the appropriate duty of care has been breached. In *Latimer v AEC Ltd* (1953) the floor of the defendant's factory was flooded by an exceptionally heavy rainstorm. Oil which was kept in troughs was washed out on to the factory floor. The defendant put sawdust on the floor but there was not enough sawdust to cover the entire factory floor. The plaintiff, who was working on the floor, slipped and injured himself. He sued the defendant. It was held that the defendant was not liable since he had taken all appropriate precautions short of closing the factory. However, this decision has been criticised on the ground that commercial profitability was given too much prominence by the court over the personal security of the workers. It may well be that on similar facts a court would reach a different decision today.

Emergency situations

If the defender is placed in a sudden emergency situation which is not of his own creation, his actions must be judged in the light of those circumstances. In *Ng Chun Pui* v *Lee Chuen Tat* (1988) it was held that the driver of a coach who had braked, swerved and skidded when another vehicle had cut across his path had acted in an emergency.

Children

As far as children are concerned, one takes into account what degree of care a child of the particular age of the defender can be expected to take: *Yachuk* v *Oliver Blais Co Ltd* (1949).

By way of conclusion on the subject of standard of care, it should be borne in mind that the courts have formulated special rules to determine whether professional people, such as doctors, have breached the standard of care which the law demands of them.

(3) CAUSATION

Finally, in order to succeed in a negligence claim it is necessary to prove that the negligent act in question actually caused the relevant injury or damage which is the subject-matter of the action. There are two main tests which the courts use in order to ascertain whether the defender's conduct caused the loss in question, namely:

(a) the "but for" test; and

(b) the "material contribution" test.

(a) The "but for" test

The question which the court asks itself here is: but for the negligent act of the defender, would the pursuer have been harmed? The leading case on the subject is *Barnett* v *Chelsea and Kensington Hospital Management Committee* (1969). In that case Barnett, a night watchman, called early one morning at the defendant's hospital. He had been complaining of sickness. Unbeknown to Barnett, he had been deliberately poisoned. However, the doctor in charge refused to see him and suggested that he should consult his GP in the morning. Unfortunately, Barnett died before he could visit his GP. Barnett's widow sued the hospital in negligence. However, she failed in her action since it was proved that her husband would have died in spite of any medical assistance which he could have been given at the time when he presented himself at hospital. In other words, the defendant had not caused Barnett's death.

(b) The "material contribution" test

As far as this test is concerned, the courts are willing to accept that the defender has caused the relevant damage if his negligent act materially contributes to, as opposed to being the sole cause of, the accident. The test is well illustrated in *Wardlaw* v *Bonnington Castings* (1956). In that case the pursuer's illness was caused by an accumulation of dust in his lungs. The dust in question came from two sources. The defenders (Wardlaw's employers) were not responsible for one of the sources, but they could have prevented (and were therefore negligent concerning) the other. The dust from the latter source (in other words, the "illegal" dust) was not in itself sufficient to cause the disease. However, the pursuer succeeded in his action because the "illegal" dust had made a material contribution to his injury: see also *McGhee* v *NCB* (1972).

It is also important to understand that the pursuer requires to prove on a balance of probabilities that the negligent act of the defender caused his injury: *Wilsher* v *Essex Area Health Authority* (1988).

Departure from the "rules"

In *Fairchild* v *Glenhaven Funeral Services* (2002) it was held that in certain circumstances one could depart from the well-established rules governing factual causation. In that case Fairchild had been employed at different times and for different periods by more than one employer: E1 and E2. Both E1 and E2 had been subject to a duty to take reasonable care to prevent F from inhaling asbestos dust. Both E1 and E2 failed to do so and, as a consequence, F contracted mesothelioma. On the current limits of scientific knowledge, Fairchild was unable to prove on the balance of probabilities that his condition was the result of inhaling asbestos dust during his employment by one or other or both of E1 or E2. However, the House of Lords held that, in certain special circumstances, the court could depart from the established test of legal causation and treat a lesser degree of causal connection as sufficient, namely that the defendant's breach of duty had materially contributed to causing the disease by materially increasing the risk that the disease would be contracted. Any injustice that might be involved in imposing liability in such circumstances was heavily outweighed by the injustice of denying redress to the victim.

The law was taken further in the House of Lords case of *Barker* v *Corus (UK) Ltd* (2006) in which it was held that, on facts similar to those which formed the basis of *Fairchild,* it was appropriate to apportion liability between defendants in accordance with the degree of risk to which the defendants exposed the claimant by virtue of their negligence. As far as liability in respect of mesothelioma is concerned, s 3 of the Compensation Act 2006 reverses *Barker* and makes the person who is at fault jointly and severally liable (ie *in solidum*) with any other person.

Legal causation (remoteness of damage)

The law will not allow the pursuer to recover in relation to injury which is deemed to be too remote. Consider the following scenario. Allan, a builder, negligently builds the foundations of Tom's house: the foundations are too shallow. Soon, cracks develop in the walls and the building becomes dangerous. Tom has to leave the house and move into rented accommodation in a poorer part of the town. While Tom is living there he is mugged by a gang and is injured. Could Tom sue Allan in respect of his personal injuries? The answer to that question would be that the law would probably regard his injuries as too remote. How do the courts ascertain whether the damage in question is too remote? There are two competing rules, namely:

(1) the "directness" test; and

(2) the "foreseeability" test.

(1) The "directness" test

The leading case on the directness test is *Re Polemis* (1921). In that case a chartered vessel was unloading in Casablanca. The servants of the charterers negligently let a plank of wood drop into the hold of the ship. Part of the cargo was a quantity of petrol which had leaked out of its containers. The fall of the plank caused a spark which in turn caused the petrol to explode. The ship was completely destroyed. The charterers were held liable by the Court of Appeal for the loss because such loss was the direct consequence of the act of negligence in question.

(2) The "foreseeability" test

The competing test to the "directness" test is the rule in *The Wagon Mound* (1961). In that case, OT Ltd were charterers of a ship known as the *Wagon Mound* which was moored in a wharf in Sydney, Australia. OT's servants allowed a large quantity of oil to be spilled and it spread to another wharf where another ship was under repair. Sparks from the welding operations in this other part of the harbour fell on to the water. The oil caught fire and the wharf was damaged. The Privy Council held that while the damage was the direct cause of the spillage in question, it was unforeseeable and so the defendants were not liable. The foresight of the hypothetical reasonable man in the position of the defender at the time of the accident determined liability. It is the rule in *The Wagon Mound* (1961) which is now favoured by the courts in preference to the rule in *Re Polemis* (1921) as far as remoteness of damage in negligence actions is concerned.

The "thin skull" rule

If I am walking along a pavement one day and I am gently knocked to the ground by a skateboarder and fracture my skull as a consequence because my skull is thinner and therefore more breakable than normal, the skateboarder could not argue by way of defence that my serious injury was not reasonably foreseeable. In other words, in terms of remoteness of injury the defender takes the pursuer as he finds him. This is known as the "thin skull" rule. The type of injury, namely a wound to the head, is certainly foreseeable. However, the extent of the injury is not. Under the rule I can recover the full extent of my injuries which directly derive from a state of affairs which was reasonably foreseeable.

A good illustration of the application of the "thin skull" rule is seen in *Smith* v *Leech Brain and Co* (1962). In that case the plaintiff suffered a burn on his lip as a result of the defendant's negligence. The burn caused the plaintiff to contract cancer because the tissues of his lips were in a premalignant state. He died within 3 years. The defendants argued that they were not responsible for his death as it could not have been foreseen. It was held, however, that the principle that the defendant had to "take his victim as he found him" applied. The defendants were therefore held liable.

Breaking the chain of causation

It sometimes happens that an event occurs between the negligent act of the defender and injury being sustained by the pursuer. The effect of the intervening event is to break, in the eye of the law, the link between the negligent act and the damage in question, in which case the defender would not be liable for the relevant damage. The intervening act would then eclipse the original act of negligence, as it were, and therefore negate liability in delict. The intervening act would be said to be a *novus actus interveniens*. How do the courts ascertain whether a given act falls to be dealt with as either a *novus actus interveniens* or *causa causans* (that is to say, an act which is not independent from the original act of negligence and, therefore, falls to be regarded as a link between the defender's act of negligence and the subsequent damage)? The short answer to this question is that the courts have never really felt comfortable with this particular aspect of the law of negligence and tend to approach the issue of *novus actus interveniens* on a case-by-case basis.

Sometimes, if the intervening act is the natural and reasonable consequence of the original act of negligence it breaks the chain of causation: *The Oropesa* (1943); *Rouse* v *Squires* (1973). At other times, if the intervening conduct is deemed to be unreasonable, it breaks the chain of causation. For example, in *McKew* v *Holland and Hannen and Cubitts (Scotland) Ltd* (1970) the pursuer sustained an injury in an accident which was caused by the defender's negligence. The pursuer's leg would become numb and tend to give way without warning. One day, when he was descending stairs, he felt his leg give way. The pursuer jumped to the bottom of the stairs and he sustained further injury. The House of Lords held that the pursuer had acted unreasonably in placing himself in such a position that he could do little to save himself if his leg gave way. Furthermore, such unreasonable conduct constituted a *novus actus interveniens* and therefore broke the chain of causation between the defendant's negligent act and the injury sustained by jumping down the stairs.

Finally, in some cases, foreseeability is the touchstone which is employed by the courts to ascertain whether the chain of causation has been broken. For example, in *Donaghy* v *NCB* (1957) a young miner sued his employers in respect of injuries he received when a detonator, which had been left in the pursuer's workplace in breach of relevant legislation, exploded when he hit it with a hammer. The Inner House of the Court of Session held that the act of the pursuer constituted a *novus actus interveniens* since the pursuer's act was not reasonably foreseeable.

Essential Facts

- In order to ascertain whether the defender is liable in law for damage which he has negligently caused, the court must decide whether the defender owes the pursuer a duty of care.
- Currently, the courts employ an incremental test to ascertain whether a duty of care exists.
- The court must decide whether, on the facts of the particular case, a duty of care was owed.
- The general rule is that there is no liability for pure economic loss.
- In order that one can recover for harm which is caused by a negligent statement there must be assumption of responsibility on the part of the maker of the statement and reliance on that statement.
- The courts divide victims of nervous shock into primary and secondary victims.
- A primary victim is directly involved in the relevant traumatic event.
- A secondary victim merely witnesses the event.
- In order to recover if one is a secondary victim, one must witness the events with one's own unaided senses and have a bond of love and affection with the person injured.
- Generally, the courts do not impose a duty of care for one failing to act.
- Whether the defender has failed to attain the standard of care which the law demands of him is judged objectively.
- In order to recover in negligence it must be proved that the negligent act in question caused the damage and that the injury is not too remote.

Essential Cases

Donoghue v Stevenson (1932): established the "foreseeeability" test in relation to the duty of care in the law of negligence.

Caparo v Dickman (1990): established the "incremental" test in relation to the duty of care.

Bourhill v Young (1942): illustrates the principle that it must be proved that the defender owes the pursuer a factual duty of care.

Spartan Steel and Alloys Ltd v Martin and Co (Contractors) Ltd (1972): no liability for pure economic loss.

Hedley Byrne v Heller (1964): liability lies for making of negligent statement if the maker assumes responsibility for its accuracy and the recipient relies on the statement.

Page v Smith (1996): no distinction in principle between physical and psychiatric injury as far as primary victims of nervous shock are concerned.

Alcock v Chief Constable of South Yorkshire (1991): in order to recover as a secondary victim of nervous shock, one must establish a bond of love and affection with the victim and perceive the traumatic event with one's own unaided senses.

Nettleship v Weston (1971): whether the defender has failed to attain the standard of care which the law demands of him is judged objectively.

Barnett v Chelsea and Kensington Hospital Management Committee (1969): the pursuer must prove a causal link between the defender's negligent act and the former's injury.

Wardlaw v Bonnington Castings (1956): the pursuer can succeed if he can prove the defender's negligence.

Wilsher v Essex Area Health Authority (1988): the pursuer requires to prove that the negligent act of the defender caused the former's injury on a balance of probabilities.

Fairchild v Glenhaven Funeral Services (2002): in certain circumstances one can depart from the well-established rules governing factual causation.

Barker v Corus (UK) Ltd (2006): on facts similar to those which formed the basis of *Fairchild* it is appropriate to apportion liability between defendants in accordance with the degree of risk to which the defendants exposed the claimant to by virtue of their negligence.

3   THE LAW OF NUISANCE

The law recognises the fact that if one has the right to occupy land, for example by owning or having a lease of the land in question, one has the right to enjoy that land free from external interference. However, the right to occupy land also brings with it the right to carry on lawful activities on that land. Inevitably, sometimes these rights conflict. For example, my next-door neighbour may wish to play his radio loud each night. However, I may wish to study in peace and quiet in my own house. What the law does is to attempt to strike a reasonable balance between these conflicting rights. This conflict is pragmatically resolved by the courts imposing a duty on an occupier of land not to use his land in such an unreasonable way that the enjoyment of another is prejudiced. This duty is sometimes expressed in the Latin maxim *sic utere tuo ut alienum non laedas* (so use your property that you do not harm your neighbour). The law was neatly summarised by Lord President Cooper in *Watt* v *Jamieson* (1954) when he stated:

> "The balance in all such cases has to be held between the freedom of a proprietor to use his property as he pleases and the duty on a proprietor not to inflict material loss or inconvenience on adjoining proprietors and in every case the answer depends on considerations of fact and degree."

The *Watt* decision emphasises that whether any given state of affairs constitutes an actionable nuisance is a question of fact and degree. For example, the louder the noise or the more intense the smoke which come from my neighbour's property, the more likely the courts will categorise the state of affairs as a nuisance in law.

FACTORS THE COURT TAKES INTO ACCOUNT

We now look at the various factors which require to be taken into account when considering whether a given state of affairs constitutes a nuisance in law. One should remember at the outset that it is only unreasonable conduct which can be categorised as a nuisance in law (*Baxter* v *Camden London Borough Council* (1999)). In order to ascertain whether any given conduct is unreasonable the law has traditionally focused on the relevant conduct from the viewpoint of the pursuer (*Watt* v *Jamieson* (1954)). Before we go on to itemise what factors a court takes into account, it must be stressed that the factors which are listed are not mechanically applied in every nuisance case. Rather, the courts have tended to emphasise several factors, often to the exclusion of others. Finally, it should be remembered that the factors which are listed are not exhaustive. It is open to the courts to introduce other factors.

Social utility

The social utility or benefit which is associated with the activity causing the nuisance in question is taken into account by the courts. The gist of this factor is that the more socially useful an activity is, the less likely it is that the court could be willing to castigate the state of affairs complained of as a nuisance (*Harrison* v *Southwark and Vauxhall Water Co* (1891)). Social utility has most commonly featured in the context of industrial nuisances where the courts have explicitly recognised the social benefits which accrue from factories (see, for example, *Bellew* v *Cement Ltd* (1948)).

Motive of the defender

If the relevant state of affairs is generated simply to punish the pursuer, that is to say it is motivated by spite, the courts are readily inclined to hold that the state of affairs ranks as a nuisance. For example, in the leading case of *Christie* v *Davey* (1893) the plaintiff's family were musically inclined and frequently practised their instruments to the annoyance of the defendant who retaliated by banging trays on the party wall which separated his house from that of the plaintiff. It was held that the noise which was generated by the defendant amounted to a nuisance in law because it was motivated by spite. Similarly, in *Hollywood Silver Fox Farm Ltd* v *Emmett* (1936) the plaintiff bred foxes on his land. The defendant objected to this practice and caused guns to be fired on the boundary which separated his premises from those of the plaintiff. It was held that the noise constituted a nuisance in law.

Locality

The nature of the locality has a bearing on whether a state of affairs can rank as a nuisance in law (*Trotter* v *Farnie* (1830)). The reasoning behind this approach is that if a state of affairs is typical of a given locality, the pursuer would be presumed to have become habituated, at least to some extent, to the nuisance in question. The leading case on the application of the locality factor is *Bramford* v *Turnley* (1862) where Pollock CB stated at 286: "That may be a nuisance in Grosvenor Square, which would be none in Smithfield Market." The Scottish equivalent of *Bramford* is

Inglis v *Shotts Iron Co* (1881) where the Lord Justice-Clerk stated at 1021: "Things which are forbidden in a crowded urban community may be permitted in the country. What is prohibited in enclosed land may be tolerated in the open."

However, while the courts are less inclined to castigate as a nuisance a state of affairs which is typical of an area, they are not prepared to accord the defender *carte blanche* to create a nuisance. This point was illustrated in *Rushmer* v *Polsue and Alfieri Ltd* (1906), where the House of Lords upheld the grant of an injunction in relation to noise from premises notwithstanding the fact that it was habitual practice for certain premises in the relevant area to operate their presses during the night.

It is important to note that if the adverse state of affairs injures the pursuer's property the locality principle is redundant. In *St Helens Smelting Co* v *Tipping* (1865) vapours from the defendant's works damaged the claimant's property. It was held irrelevant that the claimant's property was situated in an industrial area.

Duration and intensity

What this means is the longer an adverse state of affairs lasts and also the more intense its nature, the more likely that it will be categorised a nuisance. In the leading case of *Bamford* v *Turnley* (1862) Pollock CB stated at 292:

> "A clock striking the hour, or a bell ringing for some domestic purpose, may be a nuisance if unreasonably loud or discordant, of which the jury must alone judge; but although not unreasonably loud, if the owner from some whim or caprice made the clock strike every 10 minutes, or the bell ring continually, I think that a jury would be justified in considering it to be a very great nuisance."

Time of day

The courts are more inclined to regard night noise a nuisance than noise which takes place during the day (*Bamford* v *Turnley* (1862)). The time of day at which an adverse state of affairs exists is only applicable in relation to noise nuisances and perhaps light nuisance.

Sensitivity of the pursuer

The courts are unwilling to conclude that a nuisance exists if the pursuer is annoyed by the adverse state of affairs simply because he is oversensitive.

In *Heath* v *Brighton Corporation* (1908), a priest complained about the noise and vibrations which emanated from the defendant's premises. The claimant was denied a remedy under the law of nuisance since the sole reason why he was discomfited was because he possessed hypersensitive hearing. The rule that the courts will not provide relief by way of the law of nuisance to the oversensitive also applies in relation to physical injury to property. For example, in *Robertson* v *Kilvert* (1889) the claimant kept delicate paper in his premises. The paper was damaged by the heat which was generated from the defendant's premises. The claimant failed in his action. More recently, in *Bridlington Relay Ltd* v *Yorkshire Electricity Board* (1965) the claimant company carried on a business of providing a relay system of sound and television broadcasts and erected a mast on its own land for that purpose. The defendant local electricity board began to erect an overhead power line near the mast which would have interfered with the reception of signals. It was held that since the business of the claimant required an exceptional degree of immunity from interference, the action in nuisance failed. Similarly, in *Hunter* v *Canary Wharf Ltd* (1997), the House of Lords held that the interference with the reception of television signals by the presence of a large building did not constitute an actionable nuisance in law.

The above cases were reviewed by the Court of Appeal in *Network Rail Infrastructure Ltd (formerly Railtrack)* v *C J Morris* (2004). In that case it was claimed that Railtrack's signalling system had caused electromagnetic interference to the electric guitars which were played in the claimant's recording studios situated some 80 metres away. However, the court held that amplified guitars fell to be regarded as extraordinarily sensitive equipment which did not attract the protection of the law of nuisance.

NEED FOR AN EMANATION FROM DEFENDER'S LAND

In the vast majority of nuisance cases the relevant adverse state of affairs which is the subject-matter of the action will consist of odours, smoke and noise etc which are created on the defender's premises and, in turn, affect the pursuer. The question which we ask here, however, is whether it is, indeed, essential in the law of nuisance that there is some type of emanation from the defender's premises. There is English authority to the effect that proceedings which are confined to the defendant's premises and pose a real threat to the safety of the pursuer can rank as a nuisance in law. In *Thomson-Schwab* v *Costaki* (1956) it was held that the sight of prostitutes and their clients entering and leaving the defendant's premises could rank as a nuisance. Similarly, in *Laws* v *Florinplace* (1981) the defendants established a sex shop and cinema in the vicinity of the plaintiff's premises. The plaintiff claimed that the defendant's activities would attract undesirable customers who would threaten family life in the street, in particular that of young girls who might be met with indecent suggestions. Vinelott J was of the view that as far as liability in terms of the private law of nuisance was concerned, there was no need for a physical emanation from the defendant's premises.

The issue of whether one needs some form of physical emanation from the defender's premises was considered again in *Hunter* v *Canary Wharf Ltd* (1997) where, as mentioned above, the appellants claimed damages for interference with the reception of television signals at their home by a very tall tower. The House of Lords held that an action in nuisance failed, on the basis that the mere presence of a building which interfered with the reception of television signals could not rank as a nuisance in law. Unfortunately, there was little discussion as to whether, as far as the law of nuisance in general was concerned, an adverse state of affairs has to comprise a physical emanation from land. However, Lord Goff (at 432) was of the view that occasionally activities on the defendant's land are in themselves so offensive to neighbours can constitute an actionable nuisance.

By way of conclusion, as far as Scots law is concerned, in the absence of modern case law it is suggested that – with the possible exceptions of brothels, sex shops and the like – there requires to be some form of emanation from the defender's premises before a successful action can be brought under the law of nuisance.

Did the pursuer live in fear of the adverse state of affairs?

In *Blackburn* v *ARC Ltd* (1998) it was held that the fact that the adverse state of affairs may manifest itself at any time and without warning is a relevant consideration in determining whether a nuisance exists.

NEED TO PROVE *CULPA*

In order to succeed in a nuisance action, the pursuer requires to prove *culpa* or fault on the part of the defender (*RHM* v *Strathclyde Regional Council* (1985)). In the *RHM* case, bakery premises which belonged to the pursuer were flooded as a result of the collapse of a sewer which was under the control of the local authority defender. Food and packing materials which were stored in the bakery were damaged. The bakery raised an action against the local authority in terms of, among other

things, the law of nuisance. The House of Lords held that in order to
succeed in an action which was based on nuisance it was necessary for the
pursuer to prove *culpa* or fault on the part of the defender. Unfortunately,
the House did not discuss the concept in much detail. However, the Inner
House had an opportunity to discuss the concept of *culpa* in *Kennedy* v
Glenbelle (1996). The pursuers were the heritable proprietors and tenants
and occupiers of basement premises. The first defenders engaged the
second defenders, a firm of consulting engineers, to advise on, design,
direct and also supervise a scheme for the removal of a section or sections
of wall within their premises. The pursuers raised an action against
the defenders, claiming that as a result of the work which was carried
out in the basement, the pursuer's property had subsided. The pursuers
claimed that the carrying out of the renovation works in such a way that
the pursuer's premises were damaged amounted to nuisance in law as
well as negligence. As far as nuisance was concerned, the Inner House
essentially held that *culpa* could be proved if the defender was shown to
be negligent in the common law sense. Second, *culpa* could be established
if the defender had acted maliciously. Third, liability would lie if the
requisite state of affairs which harms the pursuer is brought about by
either the deliberate or reckless act of the defender. Fourth, liability will
lie if, through some fault of his, the defender brings into existence a state
of affairs which ranks as hazardous.

WHO MAY BE SUED FOR CREATING A NUISANCE?

(1) The person who creates the nuisance is liable in law (*Watt* v
Jamieson (1954)). He need have no interest in the land from which
the nuisance arises (*Slater* v *McLellan* (1924)).

(2) The occupier of the land from which the nuisance emanates is
normally liable in law (*Sedleigh-Denfield* v *O'Callaghan* (1940)).
However, the occupier is not liable for an adverse state of affairs
which has been created by someone else (for example, a trespasser
or by the act of nature) unless the occupier takes insufficient steps
to abate the nuisance after he becomes aware, either actually or
constructively, of the presence of the nuisance, in which case he
will be presumed to have adopted the nuisance. In *Sedleigh-Denfield*
a local authority trespassed on the defendant's land and constructed
a culvert on a ditch. One of the employees of the defendants knew
of the existence of the culvert. Furthermore, the defendants used
the culvert to get rid of water from their own property. However,

the culvert was not properly constructed and it became blocked with detritus. A heavy thunderstorm caused the ditch to flood. The plaintiff's land was flooded as a consequence. The House of Lords held the defendants liable in nuisance by virtue of having both continued and also adopting the nuisance in question. In their Lordships' view the defendants had continued the nuisance by virtue of failing to take appropriate remedial action after they had become aware (through their servant) of the existence of the nuisance. The nuisance had also been adopted by the defendants using the culvert for their own purposes.

The next important case on the subject of liability in respect of nuisances which are created by others is the interesting Privy Council case of *Goldman* v *Hargrave* (1967). Here, a tall gum tree which was 100 feet high and which was situated on the defendant's land was struck by lightning and caught fire. The tree was cut down by the defendant the following day. However, he did not take any further action to stop the fire from spreading, being content simply to allow the fire to burn itself out. Several days later, the weather changed. The wind became stronger and the air temperature increased. The fire revived and spread over the plaintiff's land which was damaged. It was held that the defendant was liable for the damage in that he had failed to remove the nuisance in question from his land. In coming to its decision the Privy Council was of the view that in determining liability for nuisance, no distinction should be drawn between man-made nuisances and natural nuisances. Furthermore, as far as the facts of the case were concerned, there was no substantive difference between the law of nuisance and the law of negligence. In deciding whether the defendant was liable one should take into account the defendant's knowledge of the hazard as well as his ability to foresee the consequences of not checking or removing it and, also, the ability to abate the nuisance. Importantly, the Privy Council held that in determining whether the defendant had failed to attain the standard of care which the law demanded of him, one should adopt a subjective approach and one would therefore take into account the resources of the defendant. One would, therefore, expect less on the part of an occupier of small premises than from one of a larger property. Similarly, less would be demanded of the infirm than of the able-bodied.

The last in the trilogy of cases is *Leakey* v *National Trust for Places of Historic or Natural Beauty* (1980). In that case the plaintiffs owned houses which were situated at the base of a steep conical hill which was owned and occupied by the defendant. Part of the side of the hill which adjoined the plaintiff's land became unstable. This state of affairs was made known to the defendant by the plaintiffs. However, no remedial action was taken by the defendant. A few weeks later there was a substantial fall of earth and tree stumps from the hill on to the plaintiff's land. The plaintiffs brought an action in nuisance. The Court of Appeal held the defendant liable. The Court followed *Goldman* and, therefore, refused to draw a distinction between an adverse state of affairs which had been foisted on the defendant by man-made activities and one which arose by way of the operation of nature.

Of fundamental importance is whether *Sedleigh-Denfield, Goldman* and *Leakey* are applicable to Scots law. There is little authority on this point. However, given the need for the pursuer to prove *culpa* on the part of the defender, it is difficult to imagine circumstances where liability could not be imposed in terms of the law of nuisance in Scotland but, on the other hand, fall to be imposed in terms of the law as enunciated in *Sedleigh-Denfield Goldman* and *Leakey*. In other words, it is suggested that the concept of *culpa* in terms of Scots law is probably wider than the degree of fault which is necessary to ground liability for failure to abate a nuisance in English law as set out in the above trilogy of cases.

(3) A landlord is not liable for every nuisance which emanates from the premises which he has leased (*Smith* v *Scott* (1973)). Rather, a landlord is liable for a nuisance only if he has either authorised the tenant to create the nuisance or if the creation of the nuisance is either the certain or a highly probable result of the tenant's occupation of the premises concerned (*Smith* v *Scott*).

(4) The licensor of the nuisance. The occupier of land may be liable for a nuisance which is created on the premises by his licensee (*White* v *Jameson* (1874)), especially if no attempt is made by the licensor either to abate or to remove the nuisance after he becomes aware of its existence. The leading case on this point is *Webster* v *Lord Advocate* (1984). In that case the pursuer claimed that the noise from the performance of the Edinburgh Military Tattoo and also the erection of scaffolding to accommodate seating for it amounted to a nuisance. It was held irrelevant that the contract between the licensees (the Tattoo Policy Committee) and the Secretary of State

for Scotland, as occupier of the Edinburgh Castle esplanade, was liable in nuisance for the noise which was caused by the erection of scaffolding (which was to be used to accommodate seating on the esplanade) since he had licensed the creation of the nuisance. It was held irrelevant that the contract between the licensees, the Tattoo Policy Committee and the Secretary of State contained a "no-nuisance" clause, since no attempt had been made by the latter to monitor or inspect the activities of the licensee or to enforce the clause. It is, therefore, possible that a licensor could escape liability in nuisance for the conduct of his licensee if the licensor was capable of and did, indeed, take steps to enforce such a clause.

DEFENCES

Statutory authority

The basis of this defence is that if Parliament (either the Westminster or the Scottish Parliament) has sanctioned the state of affairs which constitutes the nuisance, the pursuer has no remedy in law. The defence was most commonly invoked during the course of the 19th century in relation to alleged nuisances from the operation of railways. Much of the learning on the defence of statutory authority derives from the so-called "railway cases" which are very complicated. The case law which was embodied in the railway cases was reviewed and clarified by the House of Lords in the leading case of *Allen v Gulf Oil Refining Ltd* (1981). In that case a private Act of Parliament authorised a multinational company to acquire land, which was situated in a rural area, to construct an oil refinery. However, soon after the refinery commenced operations, residents who lived in the vicinity began to complain about the smell, noise and vibration which emanated from the plant. The House of Lords held that the Act had, by necessary implication, authorised both the construction and also the operation of the refinery, the inevitable consequence of which was the creation of the nuisance in question. The plaintiffs, therefore, failed in their action.

However, the defence of statutory authority does not operate if the relevant activities are carried out negligently. If the relevant statute authorises the relevant activity to be carried out without causing a nuisance the defence of statutory authority is inapplicable if the activity is carried on in such a manner as to cause a nuisance: *Metropolitan Asylum District Managers v Hill* (1881).

Prescription

The basic rule here is that the law will not give a remedy in favour of the pursuer who has failed to complain for 20 years or more in the face of a nuisance (*Duncan* v *Earl of Moray* (1809)). In order for the defence to succeed, the nuisance must have remained substantially constant over the prescriptive period and also have been an actionable nuisance over that period (*Sturges* v *Bridgman* (1879)). Also, the pursuer must have had either actual or constructive knowledge of the nuisance (*Liverpool Corporation* v *Coghill and Son* (1918)). The prescriptive period begins when the pursuer could have raised a successful action against the defender. However, even if the defender does acquire a prescriptive right to continue a nuisance, he does not thereby acquire the right to create another nuisance or to increase the intensity of the state of affairs in respect of which the prescriptive right has been acquired (*Baxendale* v *MacMurray* (1867)).

Acquiescence

The pursuer may also lose his right to raise an action in nuisance if he acquiesces in the face of a nuisance. The defence of acquiescence is separate from that of prescription (*Collins* v *Hamilton* (1837)). For the defence to succeed, there requires to be a clear, unequivocal and positive act on the part of the pursuer which indicates that he has consented to the nuisance in question. The person who is alleged to have acquiesced is required to have had both full knowledge of and also the power to stop the nuisance in question (*Earl of Kintore* v *Pirie* (1903)). Mere silence in the face of the nuisance is insufficient to ground the defence (*Cowan* v *Kinnaird* (1865)). However, occupation of the land which is affected by the nuisance, coupled with the knowledge of the existence of the nuisance, is capable of raising the presumption that the pursuer has acquiesced (*Colville* v *Middleton* (1817)). Also, the longer the pursuer remains impassive in the face of the nuisance, the stronger is the presumption that he has acquiesced in its face. Importantly, it must also be shown that the works whence the nuisance arises have been erected at great expense or, alternately, that the works cannot be undone (*Muirhead* v *Glasgow Highland Society* (1864)). It must be stated that this aspect of the law of acquiescence is a grey area of law on which there is little 20th-century authority.

Finally, if the court decides that the pursuer has acquiesced in the face of a nuisance, his successors in title are also denied a remedy. That is to say, the defence of acquiescence runs with the land which is affected by the nuisance.

REMEDIES

The pursuer requires to have a proprietary interest in the land which is affected by the relevant nuisance before he can raise an action. It is insufficient that the person concerned simply resides in the premises concerned (*Hunter* v *Canary Wharf Ltd* (1997).

The remedies of damages, interdict and declarator which apply generally in Scots law apply to the law of nuisance.

Essential Facts

- The law of nuisance protects the enjoyment of the occupier of land from unreasonable interference which takes place outside that land.
- The courts take a variety of factors into account when determining whether a nuisance exists, namely the social utility of the defender's conduct, the motive of the defender, the nature of the locality, duration and intensity, time of day, sensitivity of pursuer and social utility of thing interfered with.
- Normally, there will require to be some form of emanation from the defender's premises.
- The pursuer requires to prove *culpa* or fault on the part of the defender.
- The author of the nuisance is liable.
- The occupier of the land from which the nuisance emanates is liable.
- A landlord is not liable for every nuisance which emanates from the premises which he has leased.
- The licensor of the relevant nuisance may be liable.
- If Parliament has sanctioned the very state of affairs which constitutes the nuisance, that is a complete defence in a nuisance action.
- The law will not give a remedy in favour of a pursuer who has failed to complain for 20 years or more in the face of a nuisance.
- The pursuer may also lose his right to raise an action in nuisance if he acquiesces in the face of it.
- In order to raise an action in nuisance the pursuer requires to have an interest in the land which is affected by the relevant nuisance.
- The remedies of damages, interdict and declarator are applicable in the law of nuisance.

Essential Cases

Watt v Jamieson (1954): the law must strike a balance between the right of the proprietor of land to do as he pleases on that land and the right of his neighbour not to be adversely affected by what the former does on his land. Whether an adverse state of affairs ranks as a nuisance is a question of fact and degree.

Baxter v Camden LBC (1999): in order to ascertain whether a given state of affairs ranks as a nuisance, one approaches the issue from the viewpoint of the defender.

Kennedy v Glenbelle Ltd (1996): in Scots law it is essential that the pursuer proves *culpa* or blame on the part of the defender. The concept of *culpa* is wider than that of negligence.

4 OCCUPIER'S LIABILITY

Land may become dangerous by virtue of its physical state. For example, a field which is located in an area where mining took place may contain several deep pits which have been caused by subsidence. Land may also present a danger to the public by virtue of an activity which takes place on the land. For example, a field may be crossed by a railway line or electricity pylons both of which could present a potential danger to those who visit the field.

By the end of the 19th century it had been established that the occupier of land owed a duty of care in certain circumstances to those who visited the land. However, the law was very complicated and remained so until it was reformed by the Occupiers' Liability (Scotland) Act 1960. The Act varies the rules of the common law in determining the duty of care occupiers of land or other premises are required to take by virtue of their occupation or control of premises in relation to dangers which are posed due to the state of premises: s 1. It should be noted that the authority of case law decided prior to the passing of the Act is not negated. Indeed, s 1 goes on to provide that the Act does not alter the common law rules which determine the person by whom a duty to show care is owed (ie who occupies the relevant land in the eye of the law). The scope of the Act is not confined to those who occupy land (ie heritable property). Rather, it extends to those who occupy or have control of any fixed or moveable structure, including any vessel, vehicle or aircraft. However, the Act does not apply to roads, streets etc: *Lamont* v *Monklands DC* (1992).

There can be more than one occupier of land for the purposes of the Act: *Mallon* v *Spook Erections Ltd* (1993). As far as having the "occupation or control" of premises is concerned, in *Telfer* v *Glasgow DC* (1974) a vacant property was in the course of being sold by the Co-operative Society (Co-op) to Glasgow District Council (GDC). Both the Co-op and GDC were sued in respect of injuries which the pursuer received on the premises. It was held that the fact that the Co-op had the keys to the premises and the *de facto* power to exclude others meant that the Co-op occupied the premises for the purposes of the Act.

Finally, it is important to note that the Act places a duty of care on occupiers to all persons entering the relevant premises irrespective of their status. For example, no distinction is drawn in the Act between those who are lawfully on the relevant premises and those who are not.

WHAT DUTY IS OWED BY THE OCCUPIER?

Section 2(1) of the 1960 Act provides that:

> "The care which an occupier of premises is required, by reason of his occupation or control of the premises, to show towards a person entering thereon in respect of dangers which are due to the state of the premises or to anything done or omitted to be done on them and for which the occupier is in law responsible except in so far as he is entitled to and does extend, restrict or modify or exclude by agreement his obligations towards that person, be such care as in all the circumstances of the case is reasonable to see that that person will not suffer injury or damage by reason of any such danger."

Dangers due to the state of the premises

The expression "due to the state of the premises" covers a wide variety of situations such as dangers which arise from the dilapidated state of the premises to slippery floors, dry rot and poisonous berries: *Taylor* v *Glasgow Corporation* (1922). It should be emphasised that liability stems from the state of the relevant premises in contradistinction to what the pursuer wishes to do on the premises. This point was emphasised in *Lewis* v *National Assembly of Wales* (2008). There, the claimant (L), who was 14 at the time, was injured while riding a motorcycle on land which was owned and occupied by the defendant. The land had been used by motorcyclists for some years without objection from the Assembly. The land in question comprised a straight stretch of disused single carriageway which ended with a bund about 1 metre high. Behind the bund there was a wide ditch. L was injured as he attempted to negotiate the bund and the ditch. He claimed that the land was inherently dangerous. It was held that his injury was not caused by the state of the premises but, rather, by the use which L chose to make of the premises.

Reasonable in the circumstances

The occupier is required to do only that which is reasonable in the circumstances. In *Lewis* v *Six Continents plc* (2005) it was held that a hotel proprietor was not liable for head injuries which were sustained by a guest as a result of his falling out of a window. Again, in *McGlone* v *British Railways Board* (1966) a boy, aged 12, climbed up an electricity transformer which belonged to the British Railways Board. The transformer was surrounded on three sides by a large fence and on the other side by a railway. Furthermore, the gap between the fence and the wall was restricted by a barbed wire fan. There were signs which said "Danger – overhead live wires". The boy was badly burned as a result of an electric shock which he sustained when he came into contact with the wires, high up in the transformer. It was held that the pursuer failed in his action since the defenders had done all that one could reasonably have demanded of them in the circumstances. Lord Pearce stated (at 12): "In a case like this an occupier does, in my view, act reasonably if he erects an obstacle which a boy must take some trouble to overcome."

It thus becomes a question of degree, to be decided in the light of common sense, how formidable the obstruction must be in a particular case. For example, in *Adams* v *Southern Electricity Board* (1993) a boy aged 15 was electrocuted after he had climbed a pole-mounted high-voltage electrical installation. He was able to do so because the relevant anti-climbing device was in a defective condition. It was held by the Court of Appeal that the Board owed him a duty of care to ensure that he was effectively prevented from climbing the pole.

In *Titchener* v *BRB* (1984) the pursuer, a girl aged 15, was struck by a train while on a busy railway line. The pursuer alleged that the Board was under a duty to maintain the fence which protected the railway line in such a condition as to prevent access to the railway line. The House of Lords held that the duty which was owed by the Board under s 2(1) of the 1960 Act was towards the particular person who entered the premises in question. Since the girl was well aware of the danger from the trains, she was deemed to have been *volenti*, that is she was deemed to have consented or agreed to run the risk of being injured (see later notes). According to Lord Fraser (at 195):

> "The existence and the extent of a duty to fence will depend on all the facts of the case, including the age and intelligence of the particular person entering the premises. The duty will tend to be higher in a question with a very young or very old person than in the question with a normally active and intelligent adult or adolescent."

Lord Fraser went on to state that the nature of the *locus* in question was also important. He also stated that possibly, if the train which hit the pursuer had been driven negligently, the defence of *volenti non fit iniuria* would not have been applicable.

In *Telfer* v *Glasgow Corporation* (1974) the pursuer (aged 10) fell through the roof of a derelict building which was situated in a working-class area. A large number of children played there. Indeed, it was a glorified playground. It was held that the defender was in breach of s 2 of the Act, on the ground that reasonable attempts should have been made to keep the premises secure. However, the pursuer was held to be 50 per cent contributorily negligent. If the nature of the premises constitutes an allurement or entrapment to the young it is incumbent on the defender to take the relevant prophylactic measures. This point is illustrated in the recent sheriff court case of *Morton* v *Glasgow City Council* (2007). In that case the pursuer entered a plot of ground by means of an unlocked gate in which a block of tenement houses were situated and around which the defenders had erected scaffolding. The pursuer (then aged 14) climbed up the scaffolding and fell to the ground, thereby injuring himself. The sheriff held that since the presence of the scaffolding constituted an allurement to young persons, effective measures ought to have been taken to protect them from associated dangers.

Hill v *Lovett* (1992) provides an interesting example of the application of the Act. Here, a veterinary surgeon's receptionist was given permission by her employer to enter a private garden (which belonged to her employer) for the purpose of cleaning surgery windows. While in the garden she was bitten on the leg by a dog which was owned by her employer. The bite, which was ostensibly fairly minor in nature, had, ultimately, disastrous consequences. It was held that her employer, the occupier of the garden, owed her a duty of care in law.

Liability under the Act also extends to the failure on the part of the occupier to take into account the reasonably foreseeable actions of others. In *Hosie* v *Arbroath FC* (1978) football fans deliberately pushed down a gate (which was in a potentially dangerous condition) in the defender's stadium in order to gain access to it. Unfortunately, the gate fell on and crushed the pursuer who was severely injured. It was held that the defender was liable under the Act since the actions of the fans were reasonably foreseeable.

The defender need not provide protection against obvious danger on his land which arises from a natural feature such as a lake or a cliff: *Tomlinson* v *Congleton Borough Council* (2004). See also *Fegan* v *Highland Regional Council* (2007). *Evans* v *Kosmar Villa Holidays* (2007) is authority for the proposition that there is no duty to protect the pursuer against obvious dangers whether natural or man-made.

LANDLORD'S LIABILITY

Section 3 of the 1960 Act places on a landlord a duty of care, in respect of parts of premises which have been leased, similar that pertaining to an occupier of premises in a situation under which the landlord is responsible for either the maintenance or repair of the premises.

DEFENCE

Section 2(3) of the 1960 Act preserves the defence of *volenti non fit iniuria,* that is to say that there is no liability if the pursuer has fully and freely consented to run the risk to which he has been exposed.

Essential Facts

- The Occupiers' Liability (Scotland) Act 1960 varies the rules of common law governing occupier's liability.
- The duty which an occupier of land owes in respect of dangers which are due to the state of the premises is such as is reasonable in all the circumstances.
- Landlords owe certain duties under the Act.
- The defence of *volenti non fit iniuria* applies.

Essential Cases

McGlone v BRB (1966): occupier only required to do that which is reasonable in the circumstances.

Titchener v BRB (1984): extent of duty which is owed under the Act is towards particular person who enters the premises depends on all facts of the case including the age and intelligence of the particular person entering the premises.

5 PRODUCT LIABILITY

Sometimes the products which we buy are defective. In the vast majority of cases such defects result in the consumer simply returning the product to the retailer. Occasionally, however, such defects may cause injury to the consumer or his property. For example, I may eat a piece of cake and cut my mouth while eating it because the manufacturer has negligently allowed a nail to enter a mixing vat when the cake is being made. Again, I could buy a washing machine which has a defective motor, the upshot of which is that the machine catches fire and damages my kitchen.

Until fairly recently, one could obtain redress as far as the law of delict was concerned only by invoking the common law of negligence. However, in order to invoke the law of negligence successfully, one requires to prove that the manufacturer of the product failed to attain the standard of care which the law demanded of him. In practice this may be difficult. Such difficulty prompted the EU to introduce a legal regime (Council Directive on Liability for Defective Products, No 85/374/EEC, which was transposed into UK law) which was based on strict liability, thereby rendering it unnecessary for someone who was injured by a defective product to prove negligence. Therefore, we look first at how the common law addresses harm which is caused by defective products, and, second, at how liability is dealt with under statute.

LIABILITY UNDER THE COMMON LAW

Liability in relation to liability for defective products was reviewed in the leading case of *Donoghue* v *Stevenson* (1932). In that case, the pursuer, Mrs Donoghue, claimed that she had entered a café in Paisley with her friend. Her friend purchased a bottle of ginger beer (which had been manufactured by the defender) for her consumption. She drank some of the ginger beer but as more of it was poured into her glass, the remains of a snail came out of the bottle. She alleged that she suffered both shock and also severe gastro-enteritis as a result. The House of Lords, by a majority, held that the manufacturer owed Mrs Donoghue a duty of care in the law of negligence. Lord Atkin, in enunciating the so-called "narrow rule" in the case, stated:

> "a *manufacturer* of products which he sells in such a form as to show that
> he intends them to reach the *ultimate consumer* in the form in which they
> left him with no *reasonable possibility of intermediate examination* and with

knowledge that the absence of reasonable care in the *preparation or putting up of the products* will result in an injury to the *consumer's life or property* owes a duty of care to the *consumer to take that reasonable care*" (emphasis added).

The extension of the narrow rule in *Donoghue* v *Stevenson*

The narrow rule has been extended by the courts over the years. We shall now see how this has been done.

Liability of manufacturers

Manufacturer's liability has been extended widely to include those who repair and supply products (*Herschal* v *Stewart and Ardern Ltd* (1940)); fitters (*Malfroot* v *Noxal Ltd* (1935)); the erectors of tombstones (*Brown* v *Cotterill* (1934)); the installers of electrical equipment (*Eccles* v *Cross and McIlwham* (1938)); buildings (*Anns* v *Merton* (1978)); and a hot water bottle (*Steer* v *Durable Rubber Co* (1958)). The product itself need not have been manufactured negligently. It may have been rendered dangerous for the consumer to use in the absence of instructions and warnings (*Webber* v *McCausland* (1948)).

Ultimate consumer

The courts have extended the expression "ultimate consumer" to include the ultimate user of the article (*Grant* v *Australian Knitting Mills* (1936)); anyone into whose hands the article might pass (*Barnett* v *Packer* (1940)); and also anyone who is in close proximity to the article in question (*Brown* v *Cotterill* (1934)).

Sale

The product in question does not need to be sold in order for liability to lie (*Hawkins* v *Coulsdon and Purley UDC* (1954)).

Intermediate examination

In *Donoghue* v *Stevenson* (1932) Lord Atkin stated that the liability of manufacturers depended on there being no reasonable possibility of intermediate examination. However, the courts have subsequently adopted a different approach. "Possibility" now should be interpreted as "probability" (*Haseldine* v *C A Daw* (1941)).

Preparation and design

In addition to obvious defects such as the extraneous matter which is contained in the product in question, the relevant defect may consist of

a defect in design (*Hindustan SS Co* v *Siemens Bros and Co Ltd* (1955));
an inadequacy in the container of the product in question (*Bates* v *Batey*
(1913)); and also the inadequacy of a label on the container or an advert
which pertains to the product which fails to warn of the dangers of the
product (*Buchan* v *Ortho Pharmaceutical (Canada) Ltd* v *North America
Cyanamid Ltd* (1958)).

Consumer's life or property

The defender will be liable in relation to a product defect which causes
the person who either uses or consumes the product to become ill
(*Donoghue* v *Stevenson* (1932)) or injured (*Brown* v *Cotterill* (1934)).

Owes a duty ... to take that reasonable care

It is the latency of the defect in contrast to the potential harm which is
posed by the product which is covered by the narrow rule. In *McTear* v
Imperial Tobacco Ltd (2005) the pursuer claimed that her deceased husband
had died from lung cancer which had been caused by consuming cigarettes
manufactured by the defenders. It was held in the Outer House that the
cigarettes in question were not defective products within the meaning
of the narrow rule in *Donoghue* v *Stevenson* (1932) because the cigarettes
did not contain some extraneous substance as a result of manufacturing
error. In effect, the defender intended to manufacture the cigarettes in
the very form and state in which they reached the deceased. The latter,
in turn, received the very product which he wished to purchase and
proceeded to consume it in the manner in which cigarettes are intended
to be consumed. Furthermore, the cigarettes met public expectation. In
the last analysis, the cigarettes could not be said to be defective.

In some circumstances the manufacturer is under a duty to warn
the consumer of a danger which is associated with the product. It is a
question of fact and degree in every case whether a manufacturer has
given sufficient warning (*Re Children's Drink* (1993)) in relation to the
dangers which any particular product may pose to the consumer (*Lewis* v
University of Bristol (1999)).

However, the duty to warn arises only if there is a foreseeable risk that
the consumer will be led to believe that something is safe when it is not.
Provided that the ordinary consumer is in a position to make an informed
choice, there is no duty to warn of any dangers which are associated with
the use of the product (*McTear* v *Imperial Tobacco Ltd* (2005)). There is
no duty to warn of risks of which it would be reasonable to expect an
ordinary consumer to be aware. In *McTear* the pursuer averred that the
defenders owed her late husband a duty of care to warn him of the dangers

which were associated with smoking. It was held that since the products in question carried no hidden danger, the defenders were not under a duty to give any warnings about the product. Furthermore, the public awareness that smoking was linked with health risks and, in particular lung cancer, was so widespread that the defenders had no duty to give warnings about it.

LIABILITY UNDER THE CONSUMER PROTECTION ACT 1987

What is a "product"?

The 1987 Act defines the expression "product" widely. A product is defined as any goods or electricity and includes a product which is comprised in another product whether by virtue of being a component part or raw material or otherwise (s 1(2)). Therefore, in a complex product such as a television, a defective "chip" would rank as a product as well as the television itself.

Liability under the Act

Under s 2(1) of the 1987 Act it is provided that where any damage is caused wholly or partly by a defect in a product the following persons are liable for the damage:

(a) the producer of the product;

(b) any person who, by putting his name on the product or using a trade mark or other distinguishing mark in relation to the product, has held himself out to be the producer of the product;

(c) any person who has imported the product into a Member State from a place outside the Member States in order, in the course of any business of his, to supply it to another.

Liability under the statute is strict but not absolute (*A* v *National Blood Authority* (2001)). In sharp contrast to the position under the common law, there is no need for the pursuer to prove negligence.

Producers

The expression "producer" of the product is defined in s 1(2) as:

(a) the person who manufactured it;

(b) in the case of a substance which has not been manufactured but has been won or abstracted, the person who won or abstracted it;

(c) in the case of a product which has not been manufactured, won or abstracted but essential characteristics of which are attributable to an industrial or other process which has been carried out (for example, in relation to agricultural produce) the person who carried out that process.

Paragraph (a) needs little comment. As far as paragraph (b) is concerned, examples would include a mining company which abstracted coal from an opencast mine or those who abstract mineral water from an underground source. Such individuals would rank as producers and would be liable for any relevant defects in the product.

Under paragraph (c) a fish curer, for example, would be liable for any harmful preservatives which are used in smoking fish. However, it is not necessary that the relevant defect derives from the process in question: for example, the fish curer would be liable for injury which is caused by a fishing hook which is embedded in the flesh of the fish.

"Those holding themselves out as producers"

The rationale of making those who hold themselves out as producers is that consumers tend to rely on the reputation of certain companies and organisations. It is the very act of those who hold themselves out as producers which makes them liable under the Act. Therefore, it is quite irrelevant whether consumers were under the impression that a so-called "own-brander" actually produced the product.

"Importers"

Any person who imports a product into a Member State from a place which is outside the EU is also liable. Therefore, even if the non-EU producer cannot be sued, the importer of the product into the EU can be.

Liability of suppliers

Primarily liability for defective products lies with the producer. However, it may be difficult at times to identify the producer. Therefore, the 1987 Act provides that where any damage is caused wholly or partly by a defect in the product any person who supplied the product is liable if the person who suffered the damage requests the supplier to identify the producer, "own-brander" or importer and the supplier fails to comply with the request within a reasonable period (s 2(3)).

Meaning of "defect"

There is a defect in a product if the safety of the product is not such as persons are entitled to expect and for those purposes "safety" in relation to a product includes safety with respect to products comprised in that product and safety in the context of risks of damage to property, as well as in the context of risks of death or personal injury (s 3(1)). In determining what persons generally are entitled to expect in relation to a product, all circumstances are required to be taken into account, including:

(a) the manner in which, and purposes for which, the product has been marketed, its get up, the use of any mark in relation to the product and any instructions for, or warnings with respect to, doing or refraining from doing anything with or in relation to the product;

(b) what may reasonably be expected to be done with or in relation to the product;

(c) the time when the product was supplied by its producer to another (s 3(2)).

The test as to whether the product is defective is objective (*Worsley* v *Tambrands Ltd* (2000)). The pursuer requires to prove on a balance of probabilities that the product is defective (*Foster* v *Biosil* (2001)). While there is no need for the pursuer to establish fault on the part of the defender, the pursuer must show that the relevant injury or damage was caused by the defect in question (*Richardson* v *LRC Products Ltd* (2000)). However, a product is not defective because its common attributes are such that a risk of injury is posed to persons who use such items improperly (*A* v *National Blood Authority* (2001)). For example, it has been held that a disposable cup which contains a hot beverage which was securely covered by a lid that could, nonetheless, be dislodged if the cup fell and struck a hard surface was not a defective product: since people generally know that if a hot drink is spilled a serious injury may result, the risk is obvious and the cup is not defective (*B* v *McDonald's Restaurants Ltd* (2002)). It should be noted that the safety of the product in question is what the public in general are *entitled* to expect in contrast to what the public *actually* expect. The test is objective. In the last analysis, the court decides what the public is entitled to expect (*A* v *National Blood Authority* (2001)). The court decides whether that expectation is fulfilled in respect of the actual product which has injured the pursuer, as opposed to potential defectiveness of products of that genus or type. In determining what the public can legitimately expect, appropriate warnings can be taken into account (*Worsley* v *Tambrands Ltd* (2000)).

Since liability under the Act is strict, it is irrelevant that the defect in question could have been avoided by the defender (*A* v *National Blood Authority* (2001)).

In deciding whether a product is defective, the nature of the potential injury is also relevant. If the product can pose a potential threat to delicate parts of the body, such as the eye, appropriate measures require to be taken (*Abouzaid* v *Mothercare Ltd* (2001)). The Act requires the court to take into account what may reasonably be expected to be done with or in relation to the product (s 3(2)(b)). For example, the fact that a person cuts his mouth with a sharp knife while eating a piece of meat does not render the knife defective in terms of the Act, since it is not expected that a person will put a sharp knife in his mouth. In deciding what may reasonably may be expected to be done with the product, account should be taken of possible misuse by children, the elderly and the disabled, in contrast to the reasonable person.

Defences

(1) Compliance with legal requirement

It is a defence for the defender to prove that the defect in question is attributable to compliance with any requirement which is imposed by or under any enactment or with any Community obligation (s 4(1)(a)).

(2) That the defender did not supply the product in question

It is a defence that the defender did not supply the product to another (s 4(1)(b)). Section 46 of the Act defines the expression "supply" broadly and includes the selling, hiring out or lending of the goods and giving the goods as a prize or otherwise making a gift of the goods.

(3) Non-commercial supply of the product

It is a defence that the only supply of the product to another by the defender was otherwise than in the course of a business (s 4(1)(c)).

(4) Subsequent defect

It is a defence that the defect did not exist in the product at the relevant time (s 4(1)(d)). Importantly, in relation to producers, own-branders and importers the relevant time is the time when the product was supplied by them (s 4(2)(a)). In relation to the liability of others (for example, retailers) the relevant time is the time when the product was last supplied by a producer, own-brander or importer (s 4(2)(b)).

(5) State of knowledge

It is a defence that the state of scientific and technical knowledge at the relevant time was not such that a producer of products of the same description as the product in question might be expected to have discovered the defect if it had existed in his products while they were under his control (s 4(1)(e)). The defence is commonly known as the "development risk" defence.

The state of knowledge must be construed so as to include all data in the information circuit of the scientific community as a whole, bearing in mind, in the context of a reasonableness test, the actual opportunities for the information to circulate (*A* v *National Blood Authority* (2001)). The defence is not concerned with the conduct or knowledge of individual producers. The test is objective (*Commission of European Communities v UK* (1997)) and includes constructive knowledge, that is to say what the producer *ought* to know. The relevant time to assess the state of knowledge is the time when the product was put into circulation (*A* v *National Blood Authority* (2001)).

Defect in subsequent product

It is a defence if the defect in the product constituted a defect in a product (the subsequent product) in which the product had been comprised and was wholly attributable to the design of the subsequent product or to compliance by the producer of the product in question with instructions given by the producer of the subsequent product (s 4(1)(f)).

For what is the defender liable under the Act?

The defender is liable for damage which is caused wholly or partly by a defect in a product (s 2(1)). "Damage" is defined as death or personal injury or any loss of or damage to any property including land (s 5(1)). Pure economic loss is not recoverable. Furthermore, there is no liability in respect of damage which is caused to the product itself or for the loss of or any damage to the whole or part of any product which has been supplied with the relevant product comprised in it (s 5(2)). Furthermore, there is no liability in respect of loss of or damage to any property which at the time it is lost or damaged is not:

(a) of a description of property ordinarily intended for private use, occupation or consumption; and

(b) intended by the person suffering the loss or damage mainly for his own private use, occupation or consumption (s 5(3)).

Damage which is inflicted to commercial property is, therefore, not actionable. No damages can be awarded in relation to loss or damage to property if the loss or damage does not exceed £275 (s 5(4)).

It is important to note that *any* person who has suffered actionable damage can raise an action under the Act. For example, a visitor to my house could recover damages in respect of any injury which he receives from a defective television exploding in my lounge. Finally, liability under the Act cannot be excluded by any contract term, by any notice or by any other provision (s 7).

Essential Facts

- One can recover damages for defective products under the common law in terms of the narrow rule in *Donoghue* v *Stevenson* (1932).
- The rule has been expanded over the years.
- The main disadvantage with the common law is that it is often difficult to prove that the defender was negligent. Such difficulty was brought to a head by the Thalidomide tragedy.
- Pt 1 of the Consumer Protection Act 1987 introduces a regime based on strict liability for dangerous products.
- The Act gives the term "product" a wide definition.
- Liability largely falls on the producer.
- A product is defective if the safety of the product is not such as persons generally are entitled to expect.
- The test as to whether the product is defective is objective.
- It is irrelevant that the defect in question could have been avoided by the defender.
- The statute contains a number of defences, the most important and controversial being the "state of the art" defence.
- The defender is liable for damage which is caused wholly or partly by a defect in a product.
- Damage to commercial property is not actionable.
- No damages can be awarded in relation to loss or damage which does not exceed £275.

6 DEFAMATION

The vast majority of delict cases consist of the defender inflicting some form of physical harm on the pursuer or his property. In certain cases the type of harm or interest which is protected by the law of delict is more subtle in nature. This chapter concerns the protection of the pursuer's reputation. The law of defamation has two essential purposes. The first is to enable the individual to protect his reputation. The second is to preserve the right of free speech. These two purposes necessarily conflict.

PUBLICATION

In contrast to the law of England, the publication of a defamatory statement to a third party is not necessary in Scotland in order for liability to lie. In *Stuart* v *Moss* (1885) a theatre manager, Moss, engaged an actor, who was called Stuart, to perform in three towns. However, the actor failed to live up to Moss's expectation. Moss wrote to Stuart: "You advertise what you are not capable of." The words were written to Stuart alone. It was held that Moss was liable. The reason why Scots law allows the pursuer to recover for words which are published to him alone is that the Scots law of defamation derives from the *actio iniuriarum* in Roman law which allowed one to recover simply in respect of injury to one's feelings. In contrast, the basis of the English law of defamation is the protection of the claimant's reputation. Therefore, in England it is necessary that the defamatory statement is published to others. Again, in contrast to English law, there is no distinction in Scots law between words which are spoken (slander) and words which are written (libel).

WHAT IS DEFAMATORY?

In *Sim* v *Stretch* (1936), in attempting to formulate a working definition of what defamation means in law, Lord Atkin stated: "would the words tend to lower the plaintiff in the estimation of right-thinking members of society generally?". As far as the Faulks Report of 1972 was concerned, words would rank as defamatory if the words would be likely to affect persons adversely in the estimation of reasonable people generally. Generally, a defamatory statement involves some imputation against the character or reputation of the pursuer, including his business or financial reputation. The notion of lowering the reputation of the pursuer in the minds of others is a common theme.

It is a question of law as to whether the particular words are defamatory: *Gordon* v *John Leng* (1919).

Examples of what has been held to rank as defamatory include the following:

Dishonesty

It is defamatory to allege that someone is a thief, crook or swindler etc: *Harkness* v *Daily Record* (1924).

Sexual immorality etc

In *Morrison* v *Ritchie* (1902) a false birth notice was inserted in a newspaper to the effect that a child had been born to the pursuer and his wife a month after they had married. This was held to be defamatory. However, the case could be decided differently today, given the fact that unmarried couples living together is much more acceptable now than when *Morrison* was decided.

At one time, to allege that the pursuer was homosexual was clearly defamatory: *AB* v *XY* (1917). However, it may not be so today: *Quilty* v *Windsor* (1999). Similarly, an imputation of illegitimacy has been held to be defamatory in the English case of *Solomon* v *Simmons* (1954). It is doubtful whether this decision would be followed by a Scottish court today. Similarly, in the leading case of *Youssoupoff* v *Metro-Goldwyn-Mayer* (1934) it was held defamatory to say that a woman had been raped. While this case has never been overruled, it may not represent the modern law.

Improper, disgraceful or dishonourable conduct

In *McLaren* v *Robertson* (1859) it was held defamatory to allege that the pursuer was "The Greatest Liar in the World". In *McFarlane* v *Black* (1886–87) the defender contended that the pursuer, who was a parliamentary candidate, sneered at Divine Government. It was held that the jury were entitled to hold that the words were defamatory. Again, in *Cuthbert* v *Linklater* (1936) Wendy Wood, who was a prominent Scottish Nationalist, raised an action against the author Eric Linklater. In Linklater's novel Beaty Bracken removes a Union Jack from Stirling Castle and places it in a public urinal. In fact, in 1932 Wendy Wood had removed a Union Jack from Stirling Castle and thrown it to a guard. It was held defamatory to impute such conduct to the pursuer. In

Gordon v *John Leng and Co* (1919) a newspaper article alleged that the pursuer, a colonel, had ordered his men to surrender. This was held to be defamatory. Finally, in *Monson* v *Tussauds Ltd* (1894) it was held defamatory to impute that the plaintiff had committed murder.

Unfitness for occupation or profession

In *MacKellar* v *Duke of Sutherland* (1859) it was held defamatory to state that a minister was incompetent in office. Also in *McRostie* v *Ironside* (1849) it was held defamatory for the defender to state that the pursuer carried on lawsuits for the purpose of creating money for himself, in the wanton disregard of the interests of clients.

Insolvency and uncreditworthiness

To allege that the pursuer is insolvent or financially uncreditworthy is defamatory. In *Russell* v *Stubbs* (1913) it was falsely alleged that a decree in absence had been pronounced against the pursuer. It was held that this was defamatory. Again, in *AB* v *CD* (1904) the defender claimed that the pursuer, who was a solicitor, had been "cleaned out and lost his all"; this was held to be defamatory.

Unsoundness of mind

To impute unsoundness of mind is defamatory: *MacKintosh* v *Weir* (1875).

Loathsome disease

In *A* v *B* (1907) it was held defamatory to state that the pursuer was suffering from venereal disease. In the American case of *Simpson* v *Press Publishing* (1900) it was held defamatory to say that someone was suffering from leprosy. It could possibly be defamatory to say that the pursuer was suffering from AIDS or was HIV positive, even if the relevant statement made it quite clear that the condition was not acquired by way of any form of sexual misconduct on the part of the pursuer.

OBJECTIVE APPROACH

The courts adopt an objective approach to ascertaining the meaning of words. In other words, the court asks what the words would convey to an ordinary person reading the article in question: *Hunter* v *Ferguson* (1906). The court decides how the ordinary man or woman would analyse the article etc: *Lewis* v *Daily Telegraph* (1964). In order to ascertain whether the article is defamatory the court seeks to attribute to the relevant words a reasonable, natural and necessary meaning: *Russell* v *Stubbs Ltd* (1913). An interesting Scottish case where this point was illustrated was *MacLeod* v *Newsquest (Sunday Herald) Ltd* (2007) which concerned an alleged attack on a journalist by the defender. The item concerned gave an account of a ceremony at which there had been awarded "the prestigious Tartan Bollocks Award which is given to the Holyrood hack who has made the biggest gaffe of the year". The newspaper contained the following passage:

> "Angus MacLeod of the *Times* who, like Alexander Graham Bell, is justly renowned for his powers of invention, came close with his confident prediction that Jim Wallace would still be leading the Lib Dems in 2007. Mr Wallace repaid the faith shown in him by promptly announcing his retirement."

The pursuer complained that the article conveyed to the reader the false impression that he had a reputation for his powers of invention; that he was a disreputable journalist who made up stories rather than investigated them; that he was not a fit and proper person to be employed by *The Times* or the BBC; and that he had invented a conversation with Mr Wallace. However, the Lord Ordinary (Lord Macphail) held that the words complained of were not defamatory in that an ordinary reader would simply interpret the words as being written for his entertainment in a cheerful, irreverent and playful spirit and had contained elements of fantasy. It was clear from the language which was employed that the article could not be regarded as an attack upon the pursuer who therefore failed in his action.

For a recent English case where this point was re-emphasised, see *Associated Newspapers Ltd* v *Burstein* (2007).

Charleston v *News Group Newspapers Ltd* (1995) is an interesting case which illustrates these points. In that case two soap opera stars sued in respect of material published in the defendant's newspaper which depicted the claimant's faces superimposed upon two near-naked torsos who were engaged in performing a sexual act. The article which was printed beneath the picture castigated the makers of the pornographic computer game which had generated the images in question. However, the claimants contended that many readers would simply ignore the article and focus attention on the photograph. The Court of Appeal held that it was necessary to consider both the article and the picture as a whole. In the last analysis, it was held that, taken as a whole, the picture and the article were not capable of being defamatory.

It is possible that if one part of a publication says something which is disreputable of the pursuer but that is removed by the conclusion, the bane and the antidote must be taken together: *Chalmers* v *Payne* (1835). However, if a publication repeats a defamatory allegation which is made by someone else and then purports to dispel such an allegation, the publication can be deemed not to be defamatory only in the clearest of circumstances: *Jameel* v *Times Newspapers* (2004). In the leading Scottish case of *Wright and Greig* v *George Outram and Co* (1890) Lord Kyllachy stated that:

> "If a newspaper gives circulation to a slander, it is simply in the position of any other person circulating a slander, and the general rule is that a person circulating a slander is answerable equally with the author of the slander."

There is, however, an uneasy tension between the so-called "repetition rule", which dictates that a person who simply repeats a defamatory allegation is automatically liable, and the general rule which was enunciated in *Charleston*, to the effect that in order to ascertain whether an article is defamatory the article should be read as a whole. *Robertson* v *Newsquest (Sunday Herald) Ltd* (2006) is authority for the proposition that not only must one look at the article as a whole in order to ascertain the meaning of a publication, one must also look at the article as a whole in order to ascertain whether the defender has repeated a defamatory allegation.

Innuendo

Words innocent in themselves may bear some secondary defamatory meaning. For example, it may seem quite innocuous for a newspaper to report that X was seen playing football with his children in a public park. However, the words would assume a different hue if it was known that X was a parish priest! The court must examine the statement in the light of the circumstances in which the statement was made or communicated. For example, making a waxwork model of a person acquitted of a murder charge might not be defamatory. However, placing a model of the plaintiff beside a room called "The Chamber of Horrors" which contains models of convicted murderers may be defamatory: *Monson* v *Tussauds* (1894). In *Morrison* v *Ritchie* (1902) a newspaper contained an announcement of the engagement of a couple who were already married was held to be an innuendo that they had been living in sin. Again, in *Tolley* v *Fry* (1931) the defendants, who were a firm of chocolate manufacturers, published a caricature of the plaintiff who was a famous amateur golfer, depicting him playing golf in the company of a caddie who was holding up packets of the defendants' chocolate. A packet of Fry's chocolate protruded from Tolley's pocket. Below the caricature was a limerick in the following terms:

"The caddie to Tolley said, Oh Sir,
Good shot, Sir. That ball, see it go, Sir,
My word how it flies,
Like a cartet of Frys,
They're handy, they're good, and priced low, Sir."

The caricature and the limerick also described the merits of Fry's chocolate. In the last analysis, the whole publication was plainly an advertisement for the defendants' goods.

The plaintiff did not allege that the advert was defamatory in itself. Rather, he alleged that the advert bore an innuendo to the effect that the plaintiff had agreed or permitted his portrait to be exhibited for the purpose of the advertisement of the defendants' chocolate, he had done so for gain and reward and had thereby prostituted his reputation as an amateur golfer for advertising purposes. The House of Lords held that the caricature was capable of bearing such an innuendo.

Cassidy v *Daily Mirror Newspapers Ltd* (1929) illustrates the same point. Here, the defendants published in a newspaper a photograph of a racehorse owner called Cassidy and a Miss X. Alongside the photograph was an announcement that the couple had just become engaged. However, the plaintiff was known among her acquaintances as the lawful wife of Cassidy. The defendants were unaware of this fact. Mrs Cassidy successfully claimed that the publication bore an innuendo to the effect that reasonably minded people would have formed the impression that she was not the wife of Cassidy but was living with him in immoral cohabitation.

It is a matter of fact whether the words should be construed in the defamatory sense: *Fairbairn* v *SNP* (1980). It is a matter of law to determine whether the words complained of are capable of carrying an innuendo. The court must ascertain whether an innuendo can reasonably be extracted from the language which is used: *Duncan* v *Associated Scottish Newspapers Ltd* (1929).

However, facts which come to light *after* the defamatory words are published cannot be founded upon in an action which is based on an innuendo. The leading case is *Grappelli* v *Derek Block (Holdings) Ltd* (1981). The plaintiff was a musician of international repute. He employed managers or agents. The defendant arranged for the plaintiff to give concerts at various venues at specified dates. However, bookings were made without the plaintiff's authority and had to be cancelled. When informing the managers of the various concert halls where the concerts were about to take place about the cancellations, the defendant stated that Grappelli was ill and would never tour again. Later in the year, authentic notices appeared in national newspapers which gave dates of forthcoming concerts on the same dates as the cancelled ones but in different towns. The plaintiff brought an action against the defendant on the grounds that a person reading the authentic notices would form the impression that the plaintiff had given a reason for cancelling the concerts which he knew to be false. The Court of Appeal held that since the cause of action in defamation had to be known as soon as the words which were complained of were published, any extrinsic facts which were relied on to support a legal innuendo had to be known at the time of publication by those to whom they were published. Since no such extrinsic facts were known at the relevant date, the plaintiff failed in his action. Lord Denning MR emphasised the point that words cannot be made into a cause of action by reason of facts which come to the knowledge of the reader after the article etc is published.

However, if words in an article are defamatory and only the identification of the pursuer is in issue, words in the subsequent article which identify the pursuer can be founded upon in a defamation action: *Hayward* v *Thomson* (1981).

It is sufficient for the pursuer to prove that there are people who might understand the words in a defamatory sense. There is therefore no need for the pursuer to adduce evidence that some people did understand the words in such a sense: *Hough* v *London Express Newspaper Ltd* (1940).

False innuendo

Sometimes the pursuer may allege that the defender has used words which have acquired a meaning which is quite different from their literal or dictionary meaning. In such a case an innuendo must be pled by the pursuer. To say that someone is "queer" or "gay" can bear quite a different meaning from "peculiar" or "of a happy disposition", respectively. In *Allsop* v *Church of England Newspaper* (1972) a well-known journalist was described as having a "pre-occupation with the bent". This was held to be capable of being defamatory.

MODE OF COMMUNICATION

The defamatory statement need not be in words. For example, it can take the form of a cartoon (*Tolley* v *Fry* (1931)) or an effigy (*Monson* v *Tussauds* (1894)).

STATEMENT MUST BE ABOUT A PERSON

The person who is defamed must be living. In other words, one cannot recover damages in relation to defamatory words which solely reflect on the reputation of a dead person. One's reputation dies with one. In *Broom* v *Ritchie* (1904) it was held that slander of a deceased person gives no claim for solatium to his widow or children.

A juristic person such as a bank can sue under the law of defamation provided that its professional or commercial reputation is struck at: *North of Scotland Banking Co* v *Duncan* (1857); *South Hetton Coal Co* v *North Eastern News Association* (1894). However, it has been held that a local authority cannot sue in relation to defamatory words which reflect on its governing reputation, since to allow it to do so would impose both substantial and unjustifiable restrictions on freedom of expression: *Derbyshire County Council* v *Times Newspapers* (1992).

DEFAMATORY WORDS MUST REFER TO THE PURSUER

The words which are complained of must refer to the pursuer. It is an essential cause of an action of defamation that the words which are complained of should be published of the pursuer. Where the pursuer is not named, the test as to whether he is referred to is whether the words would reasonably lead people who are acquainted with the pursuer to the conclusion that he was the person who was referred to: *Knuppfer* v *London Express Newspaper Ltd* (1944). It is irrelevant that the defender did not wish to refer to the pursuer: *Hulton* v *Jones* (1910). The relevant words need not contain a key or pointer to the pursuer: *Morgan* v *Odhams Press Ltd* (1971). Furthermore, it is irrelevant that no-one believed that the relevant words were true. This form of liability may now infringe Art 10 of the ECHR which preserves the right of freedom of expression: *O'Shea* v *MGN Ltd* (2001). The Defamation Act 1996, ss 2–4 inclusive makes provision for an offer of amends etc in relation to innocent defamation.

DEFAMATION OF A CLASS

The general rule is that if one defames a class of people, this is not actionable. For example, to say that "all lawyers are thieves" is not actionable. However, if the group is small and each individual member of the group can be identified then each member of the group can sue: *Browne* v *Thomson and Co* (1912).

FALSITY

The pursuer must aver, but need not prove, that the statement is false. If the statement is defamatory it is presumed to be untrue and the defender must prove that it is true: *Jameel* v *Wall Street Journal* (2005).

DEFENCES

Veritas (Truth)

It is a complete defence to publish something which is true, no matter how hurtful it is to the pursuer. For example, if a popular newspaper were to report that a professor of law had been fined for drinking strong lager in George Square in Glasgow and this happened to be true, he would have no remedy in the law of defamation. In short, the law will not permit a man to recover damages in respect of injury to character which he does not possess: *McPherson* v *Daniels* (1829). It is irrelevant that the statement is inspired by malice. The literal truth is unnecessary. It is sufficient for the statement to be true in substance. The defender must justify the sting of the charge: *Alexander* v *N E Railway* (1865). Here, a statement in an article that the plaintiff had been convicted of travelling in a train without a ticket and had been fined £1 with 3 weeks' imprisonment in default of payment was capable of being justified by proof that he had, indeed, been convicted of the offence but the offence carried only 2 weeks' imprisonment. Under s 5 of the Defamation Act 1952:

> "In an action for defamation in respect of words containing two or more distinct charges against the pursuer a defence of justification shall not fail by reason only that the truth of every charge is not proved if the words not proved to be true do not materially injure the pursuer's reputation having regard to the truth of the remaining charges."

Under s 8 of the Rehabilitation of Offenders Act 1974 a pursuer who proves that the defender has maliciously published details of a spent conviction may recover damages.

Innocent dissemination

Under s 1 of the Defamation Act 1996 it is a defence if the defender can show that he was not the author, editor or publisher of the matter which was complained of and that he took reasonable care in relation to its publication and that he did not know or have reason to believe that what he did caused or contributed to the publication of the defamatory matter.

Offer of amends

Sections 2–4 of the Defamation Act 1996 make provision for offer of amends in relation to defendants who did not know or had no reason to believe that the statement in question referred to the claimant and was untrue and defamatory of him.

Absolute privilege

There are certain occasions in which it is for the benefit of the public that a person should be able to speak or write freely. Such a right over-rides the right not to be defamed.

Parliamentary proceedings

Statements which are made in either House and reports in *Hansard* are completely protected: Parliamentary Papers Act 1840. Provisions which are contained in an Act of the Scottish Parliament are also protected: s 17 of the Defamation Act 1996, as amended by the Scotland Act 1998. Statements which are made in proceedings of the Scottish Parliament and any publication of any statement which is authorised by the Scottish Parliament are also absolutely privileged: s 41 of the Scotland Act 1998.

Judicial proceedings

Absolute privilege attaches to all statements which are made in judicial proceedings: *Hebditch* v *MacIllwaine* (1894). However, protection does not extend to entirely irrelevant answers to a question put to a witness. In Scotland there is no absolute privilege in relation to civil proceedings: *Neill* v *Henderson* (1901). Fair and accurate reports of judicial proceedings are also absolutely privileged: s 14 of the Defamation Act 1996.

Executive matters

Communications between certain officers of state are privileged. However, it is difficult to say how high up the hierarchy the maker of the statement must be in order to be covered by absolute privilege. In *Chatterton* v *Secretary of State for India* (1895) a letter from the Secretary of State for India to his Parliamentary Under-Secretary was covered by absolute privilege.

Qualified privilege

There are circumstances in which, on grounds of public policy and convenience, the law should allow the defender to make defamatory statements of the pursuer. However, such circumstances are less compelling than those in relation to which absolute privilege applies. In contrast to defamatory statements to which absolute privilege attaches, the defence is vitiated by malice.

The categories of occasions which are covered by the defence of qualified privilege are not closed. It should also be stressed that there is some overlap between categories "(a)" and "(b)" and they should not, therefore, be regarded as hermitically sealed.

(a) Where A has a legal, moral or social duty to communicate a statement to B and B has a corresponding interest in receiving the statement, or, where A has an interest to be protected and B is under a corresponding legal, moral or social duty to protect that interest

In *Stuart* v *Bell* (1891) it was held that the question of moral or social duty was a matter for the judge. According to Lindley LJ, "moral or social duty" meant a duty which was recognised by English people of ordinary intelligence and moral principle, but at the same time not a duty which is enforceable by legal proceedings whether civil or criminal.

In the majority of cases the interest which is being protected is either a property, a business or a financial interest. However, other forms of interest have been recognised. For example, it has been held that a complaint to a bishop that a clergyman in the former's diocese had got into a fight with a schoolmaster was covered by qualified privilege: *James* v *Boston* (1846).

In *Fraser* v *Mirza* (1993) a complaint to the Chief Constable which was made about a police constable by a member of the public was held to be covered by qualified privilege. However, if the defender complains to the wrong person, he loses the defence of qualified privilege: *Beach* v *Freeson* (1972). A person who gives a job reference is covered by qualified privilege: *Farquhar* v *Neish* (1890). However, if a defamatory reference is also negligently made, it may attract liability in the law of negligence: *Spring* v *Guardian Assurance* (1995).

Statements which are made to the public at large will, generally speaking, not attract the defence of qualified privilege. However, a newspaper may be covered by qualified privilege in relation to the defamatory contents of an article which is published to the world at large: *Reynolds v Times Newspapers Ltd* (2001). In order for the defence to apply, so-called "responsible journalism" is required of the defender. The checklist (which is not exhaustive) as to whether an article is privileged depends upon a number of factors which include the seriousness of the allegation made; the nature of the allegation; the nature of the information; the source of the information; whether steps were taken to verify the information; and whether comment was sought from the pursuer. In *GKR Karate* v *Yorkshire Post Newspapers Ltd (No 2)* (2000) an article in a local newspaper about the conduct of a karate instructor was held to attract qualified privilege. See also *Grobbelaar* v *News Group Newspapers Ltd* (2001) where the claimant was a well-known football player and the *Sun* newspaper published a series of articles which alleged that he had taken bribes to fix football matches. The various publications complained of consisted of a series of vitriolic accusations. The language used was emotive and the articles had been calculated to embarrass not only the claimant but also his wife and children. It was held by the Court of Appeal that the defence of qualified privilege did not apply.

In *Jameel* v *Wall Street Journal* (2005) the Court of Appeal held, in effect, that the "responsible journalism" test enunciated in *Reynolds* was a necessary but not a sufficient requirement to allow the defence of qualified privilege to succeed. It was also necessary that the subject-matter of the publication was of such a nature that it was in the public interest that it be published. That was a more stringent test than simply that the public should be interested in receiving the information.

We have seen above in the case of *Wright and Greig* (1890) that the person who circulates a slander is equally liable with the person who defamed the pursuer in the first place. An interesting point here in the context of the *Reynolds* defence is whether a journalist who simply repeats in an article which he has written a defamatory statement which has been made by someone else can avail himself of the defence of qualified privilege. "*Reportage*" was described by Simon Brown LJ in *Al-Fagih* v *HH Saudi Research and Marketing (UK) Ltd* (2002) as a convenient word to describe the neutral reporting of attributed allegations rather than their adoption by the newspaper. The issue of *reportage* as well as the *Reynolds* defence arose again in the Court of Appeal case of *Roberts* v *Gable* (2007). In that case the claimants were two brothers who were both active members of the British National Party (BNP). The claimants complained of an article which had been published in a magazine called *Searchlight*. The offending article referred to a feud between different factions in the BNP in the London area and referred to defamatory allegations (that, *inter alia*, the first claimant had stolen money collected at a BNP rally and both claimants had threatened to torture and kneecap certain individuals) which had previously been made in another publication entitled *British Nationalist*. The defendants, the publishers of *Searchlight*, claimed that the activities of prominent members of a political party were always matters of public interest, therefore the *Reynolds* defence applied, and, furthermore, that the defendants were merely reporting allegations without either adopting or endorsing them. In other words, the offending words which were published in *Searchlight* were pure *reportage*. The court held that the repetition rule and *reportage* were not in conflict with each other. The former rule was concerned with justification (or *veritas*) and the latter was concerned with privilege. A true case of *reportage* could provide a journalist with a complete defence of qualified privilege. If the journalist does not establish the defence of qualified privilege, the repetition rule is brought into play and the journalist has to prove the truth of the defamatory words. To qualify as *reportage*, the report must have the effect of reporting not the truth of the statements but the fact that they were made. There was no need for the journalist to take steps to verify the accuracy of the allegations. The protection which is accorded by the defence of *reportage* will be lost if the journalist adopts the report and makes it his own or if he fails to report the story in a fair, disinterested and neutral way. The court went on to hold that the requirements which were listed as necessary for the special nature of *reportage* had still to be met. The court held that to satisfy the test of responsible journalism as adjusted to accommodate *reportage* there was no reason to confine the defence to "scandal-mongering". It could apply to serious allegations. The critical question was whether the public had the right to know that the relevant accusations were being made. Furthermore, in order for the defence of *reportage* to apply, there was no need for the claimant to be a public figure.

(b) Protection of a common interest

One can also avail oneself of the defence of qualified privilege if one communicates a defamatory statement in protection of an interest which is shared with the person with whom one communicates. In *Watt v Longsdon* (1930) B was a foreign manager of X Co. B wrote to Y, a director of X Co, a letter which contained gross charges of immorality, drunkenness and dishonesty on the part of the claimant who was managing director of the company abroad. B also wrote a letter to the claimant's wife along similar lines. Held that the letter to Y was covered by qualified privilege but not the letter to the claimant's wife.

(c) Statutory privilege

The common law has accorded qualified privilege to material such as accurate reports of judicial proceedings: *MacLeod* v *Justices of the Peace of Lewis* (1892). However, the importance of common law qualified privilege has been reduced by statutory qualified privilege, for example that under Sch 1 to the Defamation Act 1996.

Loss of privilege

Privilege will be lost if (a) it is exceeded or (b) the defender is prompted by malice.

(a) Excess of privilege

Statements which are quite unconnected with the main statement which is capable of attracting qualified privilege would deprive the defendant of the defence of qualified privilege. For example, in *Tuson* v *Evans* (1840) the defendant made a claim against the plaintiff for rent arrears. The defendant added: "This attempt to defraud me of the produce of land is as mean as it is dishonest." This wholly unnecessary addition deprived the defender of the defence of qualified privilege.

Privilege will also be lost if the defamatory matter is published to more persons than necessary: *De Buse* v *McCarthy* (1942).

(b) Malice

If the defamatory publication is motivated by spite or it is used for some improper motive, the defence will be lost: *Grobbelaar* (2001).

The court will be prepared to hold that the defender is motivated by malice if he does not believe in the truth of his statement or was reckless as to whether the statement was true or false, or if he told a blatant lie: *Fraser* v *Mirza* (1993). Honest belief in the veracity of one's statement will allow the defence to succeed: *Horrocks* v *Lowe* (1975). However, even if the defender thinks his statement is true, the defence of qualified privilege will be lost if the defender's main intention is to harm the pursuer. If the defender's motives are mixed, the improper motive must be the dominant one in order for the defence to be lost.

Fair comment

It is a defence if the defamatory statement is fair comment on a matter of public interest. The words must be an expression of opinion and not fact. In *Dakhyl* v *Labouchere* (1908) the plaintiff was described as a "quack of the rankest species". It was held that these words could rank as comment. The relevant comment requires to be based either on true facts or on statements which are privileged, for example statements which are made in court by a witness. Not all the facts need be stated in the comment: *Kemsley* v *Foot* (1952). However, in *Telnikoff* v *Matusevitch* (1991) a letter which was written by the defendant to the *Daily Telegraph* was highly critical of an article written by the claimant. The defendant claimed that in order to ascertain whether statements were fact or opinion one could read the article along with the letter. It was held that one could not. One could only look at the letter in order to do so.

Sometimes the defender may only be able to prove the truth of some facts. Section 6 of the Defamation Act 1952 provides that the defence of fair comment shall not fail by reason only that the truth of every allegation of fact is not proved if the expression of opinion is fair comment, having regard to such of the facts alleged or referred to in the words complained of as are proved.

The court adopts an objective test to ascertain whether the comment is fair: *Merrivale* v *Carson* (1887). Wide latitude is given to the defender. The defence fails if the defender is motivated by malice.

Fair retort

A person against whom an allegation has been made publicly is permitted to deny that charge in strong language. Judicial indulgence is given to the defender here. However, he has no *carte blanche* to defame the pursuer. For example, in *Milne* v *Walker* (1893) the pursuer wrote a letter to a newspaper in which he claimed that the defender had supplied him with inferior goods. The defender replied in such terms as to insinuate that the pursuer was a liar. It was held that the defence of fair retort was inapplicable on the basis that the defender had simply accused the pursuer of lying and could, therefore, not avail himself of the defence of fair retort.

Rixa

This defence is concerned with words which are spoken in anger. In short, the courts show some indulgence to words which are so spoken. However, there is no defence if a definite or distinct charge of crime or dishonesty is made against the pursuer: *Christie* v *Robertson* (1899).

VERBAL INJURY

The term "verbal injury" has been used since towards the end of the 19th century and has become associated with words which were not defamatory but which nevertheless harmed the pursuer: *Paterson* v *Welch* (1902). See also *Steele* v *Scottish Daily Record* (1970). In order to succeed under this head it must be shown that:

(1) the words are false;

(2) the defender intends to injure the pursuer; and

(3) the pursuer is injured.

Verbal injury includes slander of title, property and business. There is no liability if the words complained of are in defence of one's own property.

CONVICIUM

Words which are published maliciously and are calculated to bring the pursuer into public hatred or contempt have been categorised as a separate head of action. However, in the author's view this is probably not a separate head of action in Scots law: *Steele* v *Scottish Daily Record* (1970). Rather, it is simply one way of being harmed by words. *Convicium* is a form of verbal injury, it is suggested. There is little modern authority on *convicium* in Scots law.

Essential Facts

- There is no need for a defamatory statement to be published to a third party for liability to lie in Scots law.
- A defamatory statement is one which tends to lower the reputation of the pursuer in the minds of others.
- It is a question of law whether the words in question are defamatory.
- The courts adopt an objective approach in ascertaining the meaning of words.
- Words which are innocent in themselves may bear some secondary defamatory meaning. This is called an innuendo.
- The defamatory statement need not be in words.
- The person who is defamed must be living. One's reputation dies with one.
- A juristic person such as a bank can sue under the law of defamation provided that its professional reputation is struck at.
- The words which are complained of must refer to the pursuer.
- The pursuer must aver, but need not prove, that the statement is false.

- It is a complete defence to publish something which is true.
- There are certain occasions where a defamatory statement is covered by the defence of absolute privilege. Malice on the part of the defender is irrelevant.
- There are certain occasions when a defamatory statement is covered by the defence of qualified privilege. Malice on the part of the defender vitiates the defence.
- It is a defence if the defamatory statement is fair comment on a matter of public interest.

Essential Cases

Sim v Stretch (1936): definition of "defamatory".

Lewis v Daily Telegraph (1964): the court decides how the ordinary man or woman would analyse the article in question.

Tolley v Fry (1931): an advert is capable of bearing an innuendo.

Hulton v Jones (1910): irrelevant at common law that the defendant did not wish to refer to the plaintiff.

Reynolds v Times Newspapers (2001): defence of qualified privilege and articles in newspapers etc. Significance of "responsible journalism".

Kemsley v Foot (1952): defence of fair comment and substratum of fact.

7 BREACH OF CONFIDENCE

In this chapter we look at liability in the law of delict in relation to the unauthorised use of information which relates to the pursuer. For example, if I were a famous person and I gave photographs of me which were taken on my holiday to my friend, David, to simply look at and he, nevertheless, sold them to a national newspaper which proceeded to publish the photographs, would the law of delict provide me with any redress against either David or the newspaper, or against both?

In *AG* v *Observer Ltd* (1990) (the *Spycatcher* case) Lord Keith of Kinkel stated that the law has long recognised that an obligation of confidence can arise out of a particular relationships such as that of doctor and patient, priest and penitent, solicitor and client and banker and customer. Furthermore, the obligation of confidence may be imposed by an express or implied term in a contract but the obligation may also exist independently of any contract, on the basis of the equitable principle of confidence.

In *Pollard* v *Photographic Co* (1889) a photographer who had taken a negative likeness of a lady to supply her with copies for money was restrained by means of an injunction from selling or exhibiting copies, on the grounds that there was an implied contract not to use the negative for such purposes but also that such a sale or exhibition was a breach of confidence. More recently, in *Duchess of Argyll* v *Duke of Argyll* (1967) the plaintiff sought to restrain the defendant, from whom she had been divorced, from communicating to a newspaper information of an intimate nature about her and also to restrain the newspaper from publishing the information. The plaintiff succeeded in her action. The court held that a breach of confidence or trust can arise quite independently of any right of property or contract. Ungoed-Thomas J stated that there could hardly be anything more intimate or confidential than that which is involved in a matrimonial relationship or than in the mutual trust and confidences which are shared between husband and wife. Importantly, His Lordship went on to hold that an injunction could be granted to restrain the publication of confidential information not only by the person who was party to the confidence but also by others. Finally, His Lordship held that it was up to the court to decide whether the communications which were the subject-matter of the action were of such a confidential nature that they warranted protection under the law.

Several years later, liability for breach of confidence was considered in *Coco* v *A N Clark (Engineers) Ltd* (1969). In that case the manufacturer of a moped engine which was designed by Coco disclosed details of the workings of his engine to a number of potential manufacturers, including the defendant company, in order to ascertain the commercial viability of his product. However, the negotiations with the defendant company were unsuccessful. The defendant then allegedly made use of confidential information which was acquired during the discussion period in order to produce an engine which bore a similarity to Coco's engine. Coco sought an injunction in order to prevent the defendants from manufacturing their engine, on the basis that the defendants were using confidential information without consent. While there was no formal contractual agreement between Coco and the defendants, Megarry J held the defendants liable. In His Lordship's view, for one to be liable for breach of confidence, first, the information itself must have the necessary quality of confidence about it; second, that information must have been disclosed in circumstances which give rise to an obligation of confidence; and, third, the information must be used in an unauthorised way, and so cause loss or detriment to the owner of the information.

More recently, the House of Lords had the opportunity to discuss the nature and extent of the concept of breach of confidence in *Campbell* v *Mirror Group Newspapers Ltd* (2004). In that case the claimant, who was an internationally famous fashion model, volunteered information to the media about her private life. She claimed, untruthfully, that she did not take drugs. The defendant newspaper published articles which disclosed her drug addiction and the fact that she was having therapy by means of a self-help group. The articles gave details of the group meetings she was attending and also showed photographs of her in a street as she was leaving a group meeting. She accepted that the newspaper was entitled to publish the fact of her drug addiction and the fact that she was receiving treatment, but claimed that the newspaper had acted in breach of confidence by obtaining and publishing details of her therapy and the photographs which had been taken of her covertly. The newspaper denied the claim on the ground that it was entitled, in the public interest, to publish the information in order to correct the claimant's misleading statements. The newspaper also asserted that the information that it had published about her treatment was peripheral and was not sufficiently significant to amount to a breach of confidence. However, the House ruled in favour of the claimant. Lord Nicholls was of the view that the law imposes a duty of confidence whenever a person receives information which he either knows or ought to know is fairly and reasonably to be regarded as confidential. The essence of the tort was better encapsulated as misuse of private information. His Lordship went on to say that whereas formerly the action of breach of confidence was founded on some prior confidential relationship, this was not the case in the modern law. The underlying question was whether the information which was disclosed was private and not public. There had to be some interest of a private nature which the claimant wished to protect. The question one should ask was what a reasonable person of ordinary sensibilities would feel if she were placed in the same position as the claimant. The claimant's attendance at a drugs clinic was, indeed, sufficiently private to import a duty of confidence. For Baroness Hale, the important question was whether the defendant ought to know that there is a reasonable expectation that the information in question will be kept confidential.

The issue of tortious liability for breach of confidence came before the House of Lords again in *Douglas* v *Hello! Ltd (No 3)* (2008). The facts of that case were simple indeed. The first and second claimants were well-known film actors who had entered into an agreement with the third claimant, the publisher of an English celebrity magazine called *OK!* The Douglases granted *OK!* exclusive rights to publish photographs of their wedding. Wedding guests were informed that no photographs were to be taken. Also, tight security measures were put in place. However, despite those measures the wedding reception was infiltrated by a freelance photographer who surreptitiously took photographs. He then sold the exclusive right to publish the unauthorised photographs to the first defendant, *Hello!*, which was the publisher of a celebrity magazine which was in competition with the third claimant. The House of Lords held that whereas information about the wedding was information which anyone was free to communicate, the photographic images of the wedding were not publicly available and were, therefore, confidential information which warranted protection in law. A duty of confidence was owed *both* to the Douglases *and* to the publishers of *OK!* magazine.

For Lord Hoffmann, the fact that the information happened to have been about the personal life of the Douglases was irrelevant as far as the action for breach of confidence was concerned. The subject-matter of the action could have been anything which a newspaper was willing to pay for. What mattered was the fact that the Douglases, by the way in which they arranged their wedding, were in a position to impose an obligation of confidence. The Douglases were in control of the information which had commercial value.

A court will not protect information, however, if it is already in the public domain: *AG* v *Observer Ltd* (1990). This case also re-affirmed that the courts will not restrain the publication of information if it is in the public interest to do so. The so-called "public interest" defence was previously discussed in *X* v *Y* (1988). In that case certain employees of the plaintiff health authority supplied the defendant newspaper with information which was obtained from hospital records. The information identified two doctors who were carrying on general practice despite having contracted, AIDS. An article was published in the defendant's newspaper to the same effect. The defendants intended to publish a further article which identified the doctors. The plaintiffs sought an injunction to restrain the defendants from publishing the identity of the doctors. It was held, at first instance, that the public interest in preserving the confidentiality of hospital records which identified either actual or potential AIDS sufferers outweighed the public interest which was reposed in the freedom of the press to publish such information. The plaintiffs were therefore entitled to an injunction which restrained the defendants from publishing that information.

As far as the defence of public interest is concerned, the courts have been strongly influenced by Art 10 of the ECHR which guarantees freedom of expression: *Lord Advocate* v *The Scotsman* (1990).

Essential Facts

- The obligation of confidence may arise out of a particular relationship, such as those of doctor and patient, solicitor and client and husband and wife.
- The essence of the delict of breach of confidence is the misuse of private information.
- There must be some interest of a private nature which the pursuer wishes to protect.
- In determining whether a confidence has been breached one should ask how a reasonable person of ordinary sensibilities would feel in relation to the transmission of the information if he were placed in the same position as the pursuer.
- The courts will impose a duty of confidence both on the person to whom the information has been confided within a particular relationship (such as husband and wife) and also on another person who subsequently acquires such information.
- If the relevant information is already in the public domain the court will not restrain its publication.
- If the publication of the information is in the public interest the court will not restrain its publication.

Essential Cases

AG v Observer (1990): the obligation of confidence may be imposed by an express or implied term in a contract or on the independent equitable principle of confidence.

Coco v A N Clark (Engineers) Ltd (1969): for one to be liable for breach of confidence, first, the information itself must have the necessary quality of confidence; second, that information must have been disclosed in circumstances which give rise to an obligation of confidence; and, third, the information must be used in an unauthorised way and so cause loss or detriment to the owner of the information.

Campbell v MGN Ltd (2004): as far as the tort of breach of confidence is concerned, the underlying question is whether the information which is disclosed is private and not public. The question which one should ask is what a reasonable person of ordinary sensibilities would feel if placed in the same position as the claimant.

8   LIABILITY FOR ANIMALS

THE OLD LAW

At common law the person who was in charge of an animal was strictly liable for any damage which was caused by the animal if:

(a) the animal was *ferae naturae* (that is, it belonged to a dangerous species); or

(b) the animal was *mansuetae naturae* (that is, it did not belong to a dangerous species but the animal had dangerous characteristics or tendencies).

Animals which fell within category "(a)" included lions, bears, wolves, apes and monkeys: see, for example, *Burton* v *Moorhead* (1880–81). Animals which fell within category "(b)" included bulls, horses and dogs.

As far as animals which fell into category "(a)" were concerned, the law imposed strict liability for injury which was caused by such animals. As far as "(b)" was concerned, liability lay if the animal concerned had evinced vicious tendencies in the past and such tendencies were known or should have been known to the animal's owner: *Renwick* v *Rotberg* (1875) and *Fraser* v *Bell* (1887). This would include the case where the animal concerned was potentially dangerous only in a given situation. For example, in *McDonald* v *Smellie* (1903) a child was bitten by a dog which was not known to be generally vicious but had in the past behaved dangerously to children. It was held that the defender was liable.

THE MODERN LAW

The modern law which governs liability for harm which is caused by animals is now contained in the Animals (Scotland) Act 1987.

Liability for injury and harm caused by an animal

Under s 1(1) of the 1987 Act, a person is liable for any injury or damage which is caused by an animal if:

(a) at the time of the injury or damage complained of he was the keeper of the animal;

(b) the animal belonged to a species whose members generally are by virtue of their physical attributes or habits likely (unless controlled or restrained) to injure severely or kill persons or animals, or damage property to a material extent; and

(c) the injury or damage complained of is directly referable to such physical attributes or habits.

For the purposes of s 1(1)(b), "species" includes sub-species: s 1(2). It is for the court to decide whether the requirements of s 1(1)(b) are satisfied: *Foskett* v *McClymont* (1998).

Under s 5, the keeper of an animal is defined as the owner of the animal or the person who has possession of it or the person who has the actual care and control of a child under the age of 16 who owns the animal or has possession of it.

Dogs, and dangerous wild animals within the meaning of s 7(4) of the Dangerous Wild Animals Act 1976 are deemed to be likely (unless controlled or restrained) to injure severely or kill persons or animals by biting or otherwise savaging, attacking or harrying. Also cattle, horses and pigs *inter alia* are deemed to be likely to damage to a material extent land or the produce of land whether harvested or not: s 1(3).

In *Fairlie* v *Carruthers* (1996) a large frisky and boisterous dog ran up to and knocked over an old lady who broke her leg as a consequence. The pursuer sued the keeper under the 1987 Act but failed on the basis that the dog had neither harried nor attacked her. Therefore, the injury which she suffered was not directly referable to the statutorily deemed propensities of the dog.

Under s 1(4), no liability lies in respect of any injury which is caused by an animal where the injury consists of disease which is transmitted by means which are unlikely to cause severe injury other than a disease. Therefore, if a monkey in a cage in a zoo coughs on a child and thereby infects him with an illness, the zoo would not be liable. However, liability would lie if the monkey were to escape from its cage and knock the child to the ground, the upshot of which the child receives cuts to his leg and the child subsequently develops tetanus.

The "old" law and the Act

The Act only replaces strict liability under the old law which pertained to dangerous animals: s 1(8). Liability in terms of the law of negligence remains for harm which is caused by animals: *Hill* v *Lovett* (1992); *Swan* v *Andrew Minto and Son* (1998) and *Wilson* v *Donaldson* (2004).

The Act also replaces liability in terms of injury which is caused by straying livestock in terms of the Winter Herding Act 1686 and damage inflicted to dogs and poultry in terms of the Dogs Act 1906.

DEFENCES

Contributory negligence

The Act excludes liability if the injury or damage was due wholly to the fault of the person sustaining it, or, in the case of an injury sustained by an animal, the fault of a keeper of the animal: s 2(1)(a).

Volenti

The Act also excludes liability if the pursuer willingly accepted the risk of the injury which he sustained: s 2(1)(b).

Specific defences

Under s 2(1)(c) it is a defence if the person or animal who sustained injury was as a result of the relevant person or animal coming on land which was occupied by a person who was a keeper or by another person who authorised the presence on the land of the animal which caused the injury or damage; and, either:

(i) the person sustaining the injury or damage was not authorised or entitled to be on that land; or

(ii) no keeper of the animal sustaining the injury was authorised or entitled to have the animal present on that land.

As far as the defence under s 2(1)(c) is concerned, no defence lies if the animal which caused injury or damage was kept wholly or partly for the purpose of protecting persons or property unless the keeping of the animal on the premises and the use which was made of the animal was reasonable. If the animal was a guard dog within the meaning of the Guard Dogs Act 1975 no defence lies unless there was compliance with s 1 of that Act: s 2(2).

Essential Facts

- Animals (Scotland) Act 1987 replaced the common law rules governing strict liability for injury caused by dangerous animals. Liability in terms of the law of negligence remains.

- Liability lies if the animal belongs to a species whose members generally are by virtue of their physical nature (unless controlled or restrained) to injure severely or kill persons or animals or damage property to a material extent.

- Certain defences apply including that of *volenti non fit iniuria* and contributory negligence.

9 VICARIOUS LIABILITY

In this chapter we will look at the liability of employers for the actions of others. Accidents are often caused by those who are carrying out work for others. For example, an employee who performs his duties negligently may injure a fellow worker or a member of the public. Sometimes, however, an accident occurs while someone who is not an employee of another person, is carrying out work for another person. For example, a taxi driver who I have requested to take me to the railway station may negligently collide with a pedestrian on my way to the station. What has to be answered is whether the injured person can sue the person who is paying the person whose negligent conduct caused the accident in question. In short, subject to several limited exceptions, only an employer can be sued for the delicts which have been committed by his employee during the scope of his employment. One who simply pays someone to carry out work for him on an *ad hoc* basis cannot normally be sued if that person causes injury or damage. One cannot, therefore, normally be sued for a delict which is committed by an independent contractor. For example, in the example just given I would not be liable to the person who was negligently knocked down by the taxi driver since, in the eye of the law, he would rank as an independent contractor.

It must be stressed at this juncture that an employer is liable for *all* delicts of his employee, not simply those based on the negligent conduct of the employee. For example, a proprietor of a newspaper could be sued for a defamatory article in its newspaper which has been written by a journalist of the newspaper. Also, in certain cases as we shall see below, an employer can be sued for assaults which are perpetrated by employees who act as security staff.

Vicarious liability is of importance from a practical as well as an academic viewpoint in that, generally, pursuers are inclined to sue only those who are able to compensate them. For example, if I am negligently knocked over by an army private who is driving a military vehicle, it is preferable that I should sue the Crown which has much more money, of course, has much more money than the person who actually injured me. Similarly, if I am defamed in the column of a newspaper, it would be more prudent to sue the relevant newspaper proprietor rather than the journalist concerned.

It must be stressed that the law imposes vicarious liability on an employer simply by reason of his status or relationship with the person who inflicted the relevant harm. There is no requirement that the employer himself be negligent in any way for the relevant delict.

EMPLOYER'S VICARIOUS LIABILITY IN DELICT

An employer is vicariously liable for the delicts of his *employee* if the delicts are committed within the scope of the latter's employment. However, the employer is not normally liable for the delictual conduct of an *independent contractor*. This concept was well ingrained in Scots law by the early 19th century: see, for example, *Baird* v *Hamilton* (1826).

Employee or independent contractor?

We must, therefore, at the outset ascertain whether the person who actually harmed the pursuer is either an employee or an independent contractor. An employee is employed under a contract of service whereas an independent contractor is employed under a contract for services. Often it is easy to recognise a contract of service when one sees it. However, it is difficult to say wherein the distinction lies between a contract of service and a contract for services. A ship's master, a chauffeur, a reporter of a newspaper and a university lecturer are all employed under a contract of service, whereas a taxi driver and a newspaper contributor are employed under a contract for services.

    A somewhat crude distinction between an employee and an independent contractor is that whereas the former's work is integrated in the employer's business that of the latter is not. The "integration" test was first put forward by Denning LJ (as he then was) in *Stevenson, Jordan and Harrison Ltd* v *MacDonald* (1952). The test was applied in *Inglefield* v *Macey* (1967). In that case the plaintiff, who was self-employed, began to work with the defendant, a timberman. The arrangement between the two parties was that the plaintiff should retain his self-employed status. The defendant told the plaintiff what he wanted done and supplied the necessary equipment. The plaintiff did the work. The defendant did not, however, tell the plaintiff how to do the work because the former knew the plaintiff had sufficient expertise. One day the plaintiff was injured while felling a tree. Ashworth J, adopting the "integration" test, held that the plaintiff was an independent contractor since his work, although done for the business, was accessory to it and not integrated in it. While the "integration" test is superficially attractive, it may be difficult in practice to ascertain if the work of the individual in question is either integrated or, on the other hand, simply accessory to the business of the employer.

Fact or law?

In *O'Kelly* v *Trusthouse Forte* (1984) the Court of Appeal held that whether the relevant relationship falls to be categorised either as one of service or one of services is a question of law. However, it is up to the relevant court determining the issue not only to ascertain the relevant facts but also to assess them qualitatively. Only if the weight which is given by the court to a particular factor shows that the court has misdirected itself in law can an appellate court interfere with the decision.

Factors taken into account

In order to ascertain who is an employee and who is an independent contractor the courts adopt a variety of tests. The most important are:

(1) To what extent, if any, does the person who pays the other have the right to *choose* who works for him? The right to choose is more consistent with a contract of service.

(2) *Payment of wages.* The fact that the individual is in receipt of regular payment from the employer is more consistent with a contract of service.

(3) To what extent, if any, can the person who is paying *control* the manner in which the tasks which the other has to perform are carried out? The greater the degree of control, the more likely it is that the relevant relationship is that of employer–employee. However, given that employees nowadays are carrying out much more technical and esoteric tasks than in the past, this test is losing some of its currency.

(4) The right of the employer to *hire and fire* the other is more consistent with a contract of service.

FOR WHICH ACTS OF AN EMPLOYEE IS THE EMPLOYER LIABLE?

An employer is liable only for acts which are done in the course of the employee's employment. An employer will be liable for the conduct of his employees at the relevant place of employment during the hours for which the employee is employed and also as long as the employee is on the premises concerned, within reasonable limits of time of the commencement and conclusion of the shift. In *Bell* v *Blackwood, Morton and Sons* (1960) the pursuer, a woman who was in the employment of a firm of carpet manufacturers, was jostled and knocked down by a fellow employee while descending a stair after the hooter had sounded for the end of the shift. The defenders were held vicariously liable for the conduct of the negligent employee.

Frolics of employee

If an employee has gone on a frolic of his own, that is to say he has failed to carry out his duties in the manner which his employer requires; such an act on the part of the employee will take him outside the course of his employment and the employer is not liable for the cats of his employee.

Deviation from authorised route

Sometimes the "frolic" comprises the employee going on a journey of his own and being responsible for injuring someone in the course of that unauthorised journey. If the deviation by the employee from the normal or authorised journey is substantial, then the employer will not be liable. In *Storey* v *Ashton* (1869) a cart driver completed his employer's work and went to visit a relative. During the course of the journey the carter injured the plaintiff. It was held that the employer was not liable for this tort, on the basis that the employee had gone on a frolic of his own. Again, in *Hilton* v *Burton* (1961) X, H and Y were building workers who were employed at a building site. H drove them to a café 7 miles away, in order to buy tea. X was killed by the negligent driving of H. It was held that H was not acting within the scope of his employment. Again, in *Williams* v *Hemphill* (1966) a bus driver, while carrying children, made a detour at the request of some of the children. The bus was involved in a collision. A passenger was injured. It was held that the driver was still acting within the scope of his employment notwithstanding the fact that the deviation from the route which the bus driver's employers wished him to take was fairly substantial. See also *Smith* v *Stages* (1989).

Other conduct

We now ask to what extent other forms of conduct (that is, apart from a situation where the employee has deviated from a given route) can take the employee outside the scope of his employment.

For example, in *Bayley* v *Manchester and Sheffield Railway Co* (1873) a porter mistakenly thought that the plaintiff was in the wrong train. He was forcibly removed. The defendant rail company was held vicariously liable. Again, in *Century Insurance Co Ltd* v *Northern Ireland Road Transport Board* (1942) the driver of a petrol lorry struck a match while filling a tank at a petrol station. There was an explosion. Property was damaged.

The House of Lords held that the employer of the driver was liable since the driver was, in the eye of the law, still acting within the scope of his employment when the accident occurred. He was simply doing what he was employed to do, albeit in an incompetent manner. One could also say that what the driver was doing when the accident occurred was so reasonably incidental to his work that that such conduct did not take him outwith the scope of his employment. A very generous approach as to what conduct ranks as reasonably incidental to the work of the employee is seen in *Lister* v *Hesley Hall Ltd* (2001). In that case the claimant was resident in a boarding school which was owned and managed by the defendants. A warden who was employed by the defendants, without their knowledge, systematically sexually abused the claimant. The House of Lords held that there was sufficient connection between the work that the warden had been employed to do and the acts which he had committed against the claimant for those acts to be regarded as being committed within the scope of the warden's employment. The defendants were therefore liable. Again, in *Dubai Aluminium Ltd* v *Salaam* (2003) the House of Lords held that the acts of a partner of a firm of solicitors in the partner's dishonestly drafting an agreement were so closely connected to what he was authorised to do that such acts could fairly be regarded as done by him in the ordinary course of his employment.

If the employee's conduct is motivated by his desire to assist his employer, the courts will be inclined to construe such conduct as being within the scope of his employment. For example, in *Baird* v *Graham* (1852) an employer sent his servant with a horse to a fair. The servant had to put the horses up for the night. He did so in premises which were occupied by the pursuer. Unfortunately, the pursuer's horses became infected by disease which was transmitted by the horse which the servant was in charge of. It was held that the employer was liable.

Again, in *Mulholland* v *William Reid and Leys Ltd* (1958) the pursuer was killed at work by one of his employer's vans which was being driven by an apprentice who had no driving licence and was not an authorised driver. Prior to driving the van, he and another apprentice had been assisting a tradesman to move a piece of equipment into a workshop by hand. The way had been blocked by a van. The apprentice had not been instructed to drive a van but, nonetheless, he did so and in so doing killed a fellow employee. It was held that, whereas the conduct of the apprentice had not been authorised, it was sufficiently incidental to the work which he had to do to bring the negligent conduct within the scope of his employment. The apprentice was simply doing what he was employed to do in an unauthorised way. The defenders were, therefore, liable.

Assaults

The general rule is that an employer will not be liable for an assault which is perpetrated by an employee if the employee is solely motivated by spite against the person who is assaulted: *Warren* v *Henly's Ltd* (1948). However, an employer will be vicariously liable for the assault by his employee if the assault is carried out in furtherance of the business of the employer: *Daniels* v *Whetstone Entertainments* (1962). Again, in *Mattis* v *Pollock* (2003) the defendant (P) owned a night club. He employed X as a doorman. X was expected to act aggressively towards customers. One night, X grabbed a member of a group of people who were about to enter the nightclub. X was struck several times and also hit by a bottle. X then escaped to his flat from which he emerged with a knife and stabbed M who was seriously injured as a result. It was held that P was vicariously liable for the assault since X's act was so closely connected with what P either authorised or expected of X that it was fair, just and reasonable to make P vicariously liable for the assault.

Fennelly v *Connex South Eastern Ltd* (2000) is an interesting case on whether the employee is acting within the course of his employment. In that case the claimant, C, alleged that one of the defendants' employees, (S), a ticket inspector, had assaulted him at a railway station in the course of the latter's employment. The claimant had purchased a ticket and had passed through the ticket barrier. As he made his way down the steps towards the platform, S called after him and asked to see his railway ticket. C did not stop. There was an altercation during which C was offensive to S. C then walked away. S then put C in a headlock and ejected him from the station. At first instance the judge held that S had ceased to carry out his authorised role and started pursuing his own ends when C walked away and S became personally angry. S was therefore not acting within the course of his employment when he assaulted C. However, the Court of Appeal held that whether a given act was carried out in the course of the employment of the person who perpetrated the attack it was necessary to look at the job in question, and not divide out each step and task which was authorised by the employer. The initial altercation occurred as a result of S's job as a ticket inspector. The assault followed from that altercation. It was artificial to say that because C was walking away when the assault took place what happened during the assault was divorced from what preceded it. In the last analysis the assault took place during the course of S's employment.

Essential Facts

- An employer can be sued for delicts which have been committed by his employee during the course of the latter's employment.
- An employer is not normally vicariously liable for the delictual conduct of an independent contractor.
- The courts employ a number of tests in order to distinguish an employee from an independent contractor.
- An employee is employed under a contract of service whereas an independent contractor is employed under a contract for services.
- It is a question of law whether a person is employed under a contract of service or a contract of services.
- The courts adopt a variety of tests to distinguish a contract of service from a contract for sevices, namely whether one has the right to choose who works for him, the payment of wages, the right to control the other and, the right to hire and fire.
- An employer is liable only for acts which are done in the course of employment of the employee.
- An employer is not liable if the employee has gone on a frolic of his own.
- If an employee has deviated substantially from the normal or authorised journey the employer will not be liable.
- If employee is doing what he is authorised to do, albeit in an incompetent manner, the employer is still liable.
- If the employee performing an act which is reasonably incidental to what he is employed to do, the employer will be liable.
- The employer will not be liable for an assault which is perpetrated by an employee who is motivated by spite.

Essential Cases

Bell v Blackwood, Morton and Sons (1960): an employer will be liable for the conduct of his employee at the relevant place of employment during the hours for which the employee is employed and also as long as the employee is on the premises concerned within reasonable limits of time of the commencement and conclusion of the shift.

Storey v Ashton (1869): no liability if employee has gone on a frolic of his own. A cart driver went to visit a relative and injured P in the process. Held that the employer was not liable.

Century Insurance Co Ltd v Northern Ireland Road Transport Board (1942): if an employee is simply doing (although in an incompetent manner) what he is employed to do, the employer is not liable.

Lister v Hesley Hall Ltd (2001): a warden in a special boarding school systematically sexually abused a child in his care. Held that there was sufficient connection between the work which the warden had been paid to do and the acts he committed to make his employers vicariously liable for his conduct.

Mattis v Pollock (2003): an employer will be liable for the assault of his employee if the assault is carried out in furtherance of his employer's business.

10 DEFENCES

When looking at delicts such as the law of nuisance and defamation we saw that there were particular defences which were associated with these delicts. In this chapter we look at defences which apply *generally* in the law of delict.

CONTRIBUTORY NEGLIGENCE

Section 1(1) of the Law Reform (Contributory Negligence) Act 1945 provides:

> "Where a person suffers damage as a result partly of his own fault and partly of the fault of another person, or persons, a claim in respect of that damage shall not be defeated by reason of the fault of the person suffering the damage, but the damages recoverable in respect thereof shall be reduced to such an extent as the court thinks just and equitable having regard to the claimant's share and responsibility for the damage."

Essentially, the Act provides that a claim should not fail completely because the pursuer is in some way to blame for his or her injuries.

Under s 4, "damage" includes loss of life and personal injury. "Fault" means negligence, breach of statutory duty or other omission which gives rise to a liability in tort or would, apart from the Act, give rise to the defence of contributory negligence. The Act is inapplicable in relation to acts of dishonesty: *Corporacion Nacional de Chile* v *Sogemin Metals Ltd* (1997). The Act may be applicable to cases of assault: *Murphy* v *Culhane* (1977).

There are no clearly defined rules to determine what conduct on the part of the pursuer ranks as "just and equitable". Some authors have argued that the pursuer requires to be morally culpable in some way for the defence to operate. In *Quintas* v *National Smelting Co* (1961) Sellers LJ stated:

> "The respective responsibilities of the parties, and what is just and equitable having regard thereto can only properly be assessed when it has been found what the plaintiff in fact did and what the defendants failed in their duty to do."

The court determines what the total amount of damages would be if the pursuer had not been at fault and then apportions liability as a percentage of the total. If there is more than one defender liability will be apportioned between them depending upon their respective blameworthiness. In *Davies* v *Swan Motor Company Ltd* (1949) a bus ran into a lorry. Davies was killed. Both the bus driver and the lorry driver were at fault. Davies himself had been partly to blame for his injury in that when the accident took place he had been standing on the lorry sidestep contrary to instructions. It was held that Davies own negligence had contributed to his death. Damages were therefore reduced by one-fifth. The bus driver was held responsible for two-thirds of the remainder and the lorry driver responsible for the remaining one-third. Appellate courts are generally reluctant to overturn a judge's decision as to how liability should be apportioned between parties: *Porter* v *Strathclyde Regional Council* (1991).

The 1945 Act is not confined to acts of contributory "negligence". The Act also applies to a situation where the pursuer intends to do injury to himself. In *Reeves* v *Metropolitan Police Commissioner* (2000) the claimant, who was sane at the time, committed suicide while in police custody. The House of Lords held that while defendants owed the claimant a duty of care to take reasonable measures to prevent him from harming himself, damages which were awarded to him fell to be reduced by 50 per cent.

Pursuer must contribute to damage

For the defence of contributory negligence to apply, it is essential that the pursuer's conduct contributes to the damage he sustains. For example, there may be reduction in damages where a motorcyclist fails to wear a crash helmet (*O'Connell* v *Jackson* (1972)) or where a car passenger fails to wear his seat belt (*Froom* v *Butcher* (1976)).

The pursuer need not owe the defender a duty of care for the defence to succeed: *Davies*. However, the pursuer requires to be able to foresee risk to himself and his failing to take the relevant prophylactic action. In *Jones* v *Livox Quarries Ltd* (1952) the plaintiff was riding on the tow bar of a traxcavator (a vehicle used to carry stones). There was, of course, an obvious danger of his being thrown off the vehicle. However, he was hit by a vehicle which approached from behind him. He was injured. It was claimed on his behalf that he had not contributed to his injury. However, the Court of Appeal held that the damages which were awarded to him fell to be reduced under the Act on account of his contributory negligence in that he ought reasonably to have foreseen that if he did not act as a reasonably prudent man, he might himself be hurt.

Standard of care

The standard of care applying to the defence of contributory negligence is the same as that applying generally in the law of negligence: *Billing* v *Riden* (1958). See also *Porter* v *Strathclyde RC* (1991). However, concessions are made to children. In the Privy Council case of *Yachuk* v *Oliver Blais Co Ltd* (1949) the defendant supplied the plaintiff (aged 9) with petrol. The latter used the petrol to play a game. He was badly burned. It was held that there was no contributory negligence on the part of the plaintiff since a normal child of his age could not be expected to know the properties of petrol. In *Gough* v *Thorne* (1996) a girl aged 13 was beckoned to cross a road by a lorry driver who had stopped his vehicle. She was hit by a car which overtook the lorry on the inside of the road. The Court of Appeal held that she had not been contributorily negligent in that she had behaved as any other child of her age would do in the circumstances.

Agony of "moment rule"

There is no contributory negligence if the defender has put the pursuer in a dangerous situation and damage accrues to the pursuer by virtue of him trying to extricate himself from that situation. In *Jones* v *Boyce* (1816). The plaintiff was a passenger on a coach. The coach was in danger of overturning. He jumped off the coach. It was held that there was no contributory negligence on his part. However, if the pursuer is simply threatened with personal inconvenience of a trifling kind he is not entitled to take unreasonable risks: *Adams* v *London and York Railway* (1869).

Defence to be pled

The defence of contributory negligence must be specifically pled: *Porter* v *Strathclyde RC* (1991). The defender must prove that the pursuer was at fault.

CONSENT

The defence of consent is often expressed by the Latin maxim *volenti non fit iniuria*, that is to say: no wrong is done to he who has consented. Where a person consents to run the risk of injury, he cannot thereafter claim damages in respect of the injury caused by the risk. The defence must be specifically pled. The onus of proof that the pursuer was *volenti* rests on the defender. The defence operates as a complete defence.

Nature of the defence

"It is essential before a plea of *volenti non fit injuria* could be upheld that there should be relevant averments not only to the effect that the pursuer knew of the risk of danger but that he voluntarily agreed to take the risk on himself.": *Kirkham* v *Cementation Co Ltd* (1964).

For the defence to apply, the defender requires to prove that the pursuer, with full knowledge of the nature and extent of the risk he ran, freely and voluntarily agreed to incur it. In other words, the pursuer must be both *sciens* and *volens*. In *Nettleship* v *Weston* (1971) Lord Denning MR stated:

> "Knowledge of the risk of injury is not enough. Nor is a willingness to take the risk of injury. Nothing will suffice short of an agreement to waive any claim for negligence. The plaintiff must agree either expressly or impliedly, to waive any claim for injury that may befall him due to the lack of reasonable care by the defendant, or more accurately, due to the failure of the defendant to measure up to the standard of care that the law requires of him."

In *Nettleship* the plaintiff had agreed to take the defendant out for a driving lesson. The plaintiff was injured as a result of the defendant's negligent driving. The plaintiff was held not to have been *volenti* since he had asked for, and had been given, an assurance by the defendant that she had insurance cover. The consent must be to the particular risk which is involved in the accident: *Gilmore* v *London CC* (1938). For example, in *Gleghorn* v *Oldham* (1927) a caddie was injured by a golfer who was demonstrating a shot. It was held that the simple fact of the plaintiff going on to the course did not mean that he had thereby assumed the risk of injury by the defendant's negligence.

The defence of *volenti* can never apply so as to license (or to waive potential liability) in advance of a subsequent act of negligence since the pursuer would not have full knowledge of the extent as well as the nature of the duty of care which was owed to him: *Dann* v *Hamilton* (1939). See also *Titchener* v *BRB* (1984). The defence does not apply to the defender's conduct *after* the breach in question has taken place: *Sabri-Tabrizi* v *Lothian Health Board* (1998). The pursuer had an unsuccessful sterilisation operation. She had sexual intercourse after the operation. It was held that she was not *volenti* in relation to the operation.

The defence of *volenti* is unlikely to succeed in an employer–employee situation (for example, the employee has been injured on account of his employer's negligence) since it will be assumed that the pursuer (the employee) is not truly *volenti* in that he is working under economic pressure: *Bowater* v *Rowley Regis Corp* (1944); *Smith* v *Baker and Sons* (1891).

The defence is also unlikely to succeed in relation to the injury which is sustained by someone who is attempting to perform a rescue. The leading case on this point is *Baker* v *T E Hopkins and Son Ltd* (1959). In that case the defendant company was involved in cleaning a well. In order to do so, a petrol-driven pump was used. The defendant's negligence led to the well becoming filled with carbon monoxide gas. Two employees were overcome with the fumes and collapsed. A doctor was called to the scene. He was informed that there were two men who had collapsed down the well. The doctor was advised not to go down the well for his own safety. However, he decided to do so. He was lowered into the well but found that the workers had died. He asked to be lifted to the surface but when he was being raised the rope lifting him became caught. He could not be raised further and he died. It was held that the defence of *volenti non fit iniuria* was inapplicable. However, the defence will succeed if the rescue attempt is foolhardy: *Sylvester* v *Chapman Ltd* (1935). In that case the plaintiff was mauled by a leopard when he crossed a barrier in front of the leopard's cage in order to put out a cigarette smouldering in the straw. It was held that the plaintiff was not attempting to save life or property, as there were other people in the vicinity who could have extinguished the fire without being mauled.

ILLEGALITY

The gist of this defence is that the law will not allow the pursuer to succeed in a delictual action if at the time he was injured he was engaged in an illegal activity. This principle is expressed in the Latin maxim *ex turpi causa non oritur actio*. Let us consider the following two scenarios.

First, John runs an off-licence. Five minutes after he can legally sell alcohol, and just as he is about to close his shop to the public, Robert, a regular customer, comes into the shop to purchase a crate of beer. John sells Robert the beer. As John is accompanying Robert to the door, he negligently drops the crate on John's foot which is broken. If John were to sue Robert in negligence, could the latter invoke the defence of illegality to the effect that John was performing (or had just performed) an illegal act when the accident occurred?

Second, Brian decides to stage an armed robbery of a post office. While he is making his "getaway" he trips on a hole in the carpet at the front door. He is injured as a consequence. Would the defence of illegality be applicable here?

The defence of illegality would probably be applicable in the second scenario but not in the first, on the basis that it is only the more socially reprehensible that carry the defence. The defence represents a grey area of the law. It is difficult to predict with certainty whether a court will allow it to succeed.

There is an overlap with the defences of contributory negligence and also consent (*volenti*) which have already been discussed. In the Court of Appeal case of *Murphy* v *Culhane* (1977) the defendant had pleaded guilty to the manslaughter of the plaintiff's husband. It was held that the defendant could raise all three defences because the deceased had initiated the affray with the defendant.

The defence is probably limited to criminal activity on the part of the pursuer. In *Reeves* v *Metropolitan Police Commissioner* (1999) the husband of the plaintiff committed suicide while in police custody. The defendants had failed to take the necessary precautions. The Court of Appeal held that the defence of *ex turpi causa* did not apply. Although the decision of the court on this defence could have been clearer, one factor which influenced it was that suicide is no longer a criminal offence. See also *Kirkham* v *Chief Constable of Greater Manchester Police* (1990).

In the Court of Appeal case of *Pitts* v *Hunt* (1991) both the plaintiff and the defendant had been drinking heavily prior to embarking on a motorcycle ride. The plaintiff, who was a pillion passenger, encouraged the defendant, who did not have a driving licence, to ride in a dangerous and reckless manner. The cycle was involved in an accident. The plaintiff was seriously injured and the defendant was killed. It was held that the defence of illegality precluded the plaintiff from recovering the estate of the deceased. One of the reasons which influenced the court was that in a joint illegal enterprise of this kind it was difficult to ascertain the appropriate standard of care which one demands of the defendant. Therefore, no duty of care is owed by the defendant to the plaintiff in law.

Sometimes the courts simply say that it is against public policy to hold that a duty of care is owed between those who are involved in a joint criminal enterprise. This point is well illustrated in *Ashton* v *Turner* (1981). In that case the plaintiff and the defendant were making a "getaway" in a car which was being driven by the defendant, after committing a burglary. The car was involved in an accident because the defendant and plaintiff had been heavily drinking. It was held that this was a "no-duty" situation.

In ascertaining whether the defence applies, the court takes into account the degree of moral turpitude which is associated with the pursuer's conduct. In *Weir* v *Wyper* (1992) the pursuer, a girl aged 16, asked the defender (who the former knew possessed only a provisional driving licence) to drive her home. The defender drove negligently and the pursuer was injured. She sued the defender. It was held in the Outer House that the defence of illegality did not apply. Each case had to be decided on its own facts. In contrast, in *Duncan* v *Ross Harper and Murphy* (1993) the pursuer, a 19-year-old man, was injured while a passenger in a car which was being negligently driven by the defendant. The car had been stolen and the pursuer had been involved in the theft. He sued his solicitors for failing to raise an action on his behalf timeously. It was held that since the defence of illegality could have been successfully invoked by the negligent driver, the pursuer failed in his action against the solicitor. *Revill* v *Newbury* (1996) is authority for the proposition that the defence of illegality is less likely to succeed if the harm which is the subject-matter of the action has been intentionally inflicted on the pursuer. In *Revill* the plaintiff was shot and injured by the defendant while the former was raiding the defendant's allotment. It was held that the defence of illegality was inapplicable.

Finally, there must be a direct causal link between the harm which the pursuer sustains and the illegal act in relation to which the defence of illegality is invoked. This point is well illustrated in *Standard Chartered Bank* v *Pakistan National Shipping Corporation (No 2)* (2001). In that case a false bill of lading was presented by the defendants (D) to C. C discovered the fraud but nevertheless went ahead with presenting the bill to the issuing bank (X). C meanwhile paid money out. X, discovering that the bill was false, refused to pay C. C sued D in the tort of deceit. D raised the defence of illegality. The Court of Appeal rejected the defence. According to Evans LJ, there was no direct connection between the harm sustained by the pursuer and which was the subject-matter of the action, and C's illegal act.

STATUTORY AUTHORITY

The pursuer cannot successfully sue the defender if statute has authorised the harm which is complained of: *X* v *Bedfordshire County Council* (1995). The defence is most commonly invoked in relation to the law of nuisance. In *Metropolitan Asylum District* v *Hill* (1880–81) a local authority defendant was authorised by statute to erect a hospital for infectious disease. The statute provided that the defendant could erect hospitals of such a size and according to such a plan as it considered fit. A hospital was built near the plaintiff's house. He raised an action in nuisance. The House of Lords held that the local authority had no statutory authority to commit the nuisance in question since the hospital could have been erected in such a location as not to cause a nuisance. The defence of statutory authority does not apply if the defender has acted negligently: *Geddis* v *Proprietors of Bann Reservoir* (1887–88).

The leading case is now the House of Lords case of *Allen* v *Gulf Oil Refining Ltd* (1981). In that case a private Act of Parliament authorised the construction of an oil refinery. After the refinery started operating, there were complaints about smell and noise which emanated from the plant. An action in nuisance was raised against the defendants. However, it was held that since the inevitable consequence of that which was authorised was the creation of a nuisance, the defence of statutory authority applied.

DAMNUM FATALE

The defence of *damnum fatale* or, as it is sometimes known, an Act of God or *vis maior*, is very rarely invoked in Scots law. There is little modern authority on this defence. The relevant occurrence must arise from natural causes without human intervention and must go beyond anything which is reasonably foreseeable or preventable. A natural event will not rank as a *damnum fatale* simply because it rarely happens. For example, in *Caledonian Railway Company* v *Greenock Corporation* (1917) the Corporation altered the channel of a burn. During an exceptionally heavy rainfall, the burn overflowed and damaged property which belonged to the pursuer. The burn in its natural state would have carried away the water effectively. The defender argued that the heavy rainfall ranked as a *damnum fatale*. However, the House of Lords rejected this defence.

INEVITABLE ACCIDENT

The defence of inevitable accident applies when an occurrence which could not have been reasonably avoided, occurs. In *Ryan* v *Youngs* (1938) the defendants employed a man to drive a lorry. He was ostensibly in good health but, in fact, he suffered from fatty degeneration of the heart. One day he suddenly died at the wheel of his lorry. The vehicle went out of control, mounted the kerb and injured the plaintiff. It transpired that the lorry driver's death was caused by his medical condition. The Court of Appeal held that the defence of inevitable accident applied.

NECESSITY

The defence of necessity is applicable only in cases of emergency. It is a defence on which there is little modern authority. The action which is taken by the defender who invokes the defence must be reasonable or proportionate to the danger which he is attempting to counter. In *Cope v Sharpe (No 2)* (1912) the defendant trespassed on the plaintiff's land in order to prevent fire spreading to land over which his master had shooting rights. It was held that the defence of necessity was applicable.

RES IUDICATA

The defence of *res iudicata* is to the effect that the issue which is before the court has already been litigated between the same parties and has been determined by a competent court. A plea of *res iudicata* will succeed if there is identity as to:

(a) the parties;

(b) the subject-matter of the dispute; and

(c) the *media concludendi*, that is to say that the first and second suit must present one and the same ground of action.

In *Matuszczyk v NCB* (1955) a miner raised an action against the National Coal Board, claiming that the Board had failed to provide a safe system of work and that a shot firer had breached various common law duties. The defenders were absolved of liability and the pursuer failed in his action. The miner proceeded to raise a second action for the same injuries. This time he based his case on a breach of statutory duty. It was held, however, that the question which fell to be answered in the latter case was precisely that which had been answered in the first, namely whether the accident had been caused by the fault of the defender. Therefore, the defence of *res iudicata* was successfully invoked.

Essential Facts

- The court can reduce damages which are awarded to the pursuer if he has been contributorily negligent.
- Damages are reduced to the extent which the court considers is just and equitable.
- It is essential that the pursuer's conduct contributes to the damage which he sustains for the defence to apply.
- The standard of care which applies to the defence of contributory negligence is the same as that which applies generally in the law of negligence.
- Where a person consents to run the risk of injury he cannot thereafter claim damages for the injury which was caused by the risk.
- The defence operates as a complete defence.
- For the defence to apply the defender requires to prove that the pursuer, with full knowledge of the nature and extent of the risk which he ran, freely and voluntarily agreed to incur it.
- The defence of *volenti* can never apply so as to license or to waive potential liability in advance of a subsequent act of negligence.
- The defence is unlikely to succeed in an employer–employee situation.
- The law will not allow the pursuer to recover if he was involved in an illegal activity when the accident occurred.
- The defence of illegality operates as a complete defence.
- The defence is probably limited to criminal activity on the part of the pursuer.
- In ascertaining whether the defence applies, the court takes into account the degree of moral turpitude which is associated with the pursuer's conduct.
- The pursuer cannot raise an action in relation to that which Parliament has authorised.
- The defence of *damnum fatale* is rarely invoked in Scots law.
- The relevant event must arise from natural causes without human intervention and must go beyond anything which is reasonably foreseeable or preventable.
- A natural event will not rank as a *damnum fatale* simply because it rarely happens.

- The defence of inevitable accident applies when an accident which could not have been reasonably avoided occurs.
- The defence of necessity is applicable only in cases of emergency.
- The action which is taken by the defender must be reasonable or proportionate in relation to the danger which he is attempting to counter.
- The defence of *res iudicata* is to the effect that the issue which is before the court has already been litigated between the parties and has been determined by a competent court. A plea of *res iudicata* will succeed if there is identity as to the parties, the subject-matter of the dispute and the *media concludendi* (that is to say that the first and second suit must present one and the same ground of action).

Essential Cases

Quintas v National Smelting Co (1961): in relation to the defence of contributory negligence the sum which falls to be deducted from the damages which are awarded to the pursuer depends on the respective responsibilities of the parties and "what is just and equitable having regard thereto can only be assessed when it has been found what the plaintiff in fact did and what the defendants failed in their duty to do".

Froom v Butcher (1976): essential that the pursuer's conduct contributes to the damage which the pursuer sustains in order for the defence of contributory negligence to apply.

Jones v Livox Quarries Ltd (1952): for the defence to apply, the pursuer requires to be able to foresee the risk of injury to himself and his failing to take the relevant prophylactic action.

Nettleship v Weston (1971): the plaintiff agreed to take the defendant out for a driving lesson. The former was injured by virtue of the defendant's negligent driving. The plaintiff was held not to have been *volenti* since he had asked for and had been given an assurance by the defendant that she had insurance cover.

Pitts *v* Hunt (1991): both the plaintiff and the defendant had been heavily drinking prior to embarking on a motorcycle ride. The plaintiff, who was a pillion passenger, encouraged the defendant, who did not have a driving licence, to ride in a dangerous and reckless manner. The cycle was involved in an accident. The plaintiff was seriously injured and the defendant was killed. Held that the defence of illegality applied.

Allen v Gulf Oil Refining Ltd (1981): a private Act of Parliament authorised the construction of an oil refinery. After the refinery started operating, there were complaints about smell and noise from the plant. It was held that since the inevitable consequence of that which was authorised was the creation of the nuisance, the defence of statutory authority applied.

Caledonian Railway Co v Greenock Corporation (1917): a natural event will not rank as a *damnum fatale* simply because it rarely happens. The Corporation altered the channel of a burn. During an exceptionally heavy rainfall the burn overflowed and damaged property which belonged to the pursuer. The defender argued that the heavy rainfall ranked as a *damnum fatale*. The House of Lords rejected this defence.

Ryan v Youngs (1938): the defendants employed a man to drive a lorry. He was ostensibly in good health but, in fact, he suffered from fatty degeneration of the heart. One day he suddenly died at the wheel of his lorry and he injured the plaintiff. It was held that the defence of inevitable accident applied.

Cope v Sharpe (1912): the defendant trespassed on the plaintiff's land in order to prevent fire spreading to land over which his master had shooting rights. It was held that the defence of necessity was applicable.

Matuszczyk v NCB (1955): a miner raised an action against the National Coal Board, claiming that the Board had failed to provide a safe system of work and that a shot firer had breached various common law duties. The defenders were absolved of liability and the pursuer failed in his action. The miner proceeded to raise a second action for the same injuries. This time he based his case on a breach of statutory duty. It was held that the question which fell to be answered in the latter case was precisely that which was answered in the first, namely whether the accident had been caused by the fault of the defender. The defence of *res iudicata* was therefore successfully invoked.

11 REMEDIES

The main remedies as far as the law of delict is concerned, namely interdict, damages and declarator, are now discussed.

INTERDICT

In *Hay's Trustees* v *Young* (1877) Lord Gifford stated that interdict is a remedy which proceeds on the principle that prevention is better than cure and that in many cases it is more expedient to prevent a wrong from being done than simply to attempt to give redress after that wrong occurs. In *Kelso School Board* v *Hunter* (1874) Lord Deas stated that an interdict was an extraordinary remedy not to be given except for urgent reasons, and even then not as a matter of right, but only in the exercise of a sound judicial discretion.

Interdict is an appropriate remedy to prevent an existing wrong from continuing or to prevent a wrong from being done in the future where there are reasonable grounds for apprehending that a wrong is intended to be committed: *Inverurie Magistrates* v *Sorrie* (1956). An interdict is not appropriate where a wrong has been completed and there is no threat of repetition: *Associated Displays Ltd (in liquidation)* v *Turnbeam Ltd* (1988); and *Crooke* v *Scots Pictorial Publishing Co Ltd* (1906).

An interdict may be perpetual, applying without limit of time, or it may be interim and therefore designed to preserve the *status quo* in order to prevent an impending wrong. An interim interdict may be sought at any stage of a process for permanent interdict, either alone or with other legal remedies such as judicial review, declarator or damages: Scott-Robinson, *The Law of Interdict* (2nd edn, 1994) p 2.

The process of interdict is quasi-criminal, that is to say if the party who is interdicted fails to comply with the terms of the interdict he is liable to summary punishment, fine or imprisonment and may be found liable in expenses: *McIntyre* v *Sheridan* (1993). The terms of the interdict must be precise: *Webster* v *Lord Advocate* (1985). Furthermore, the terms of the interdict must be also be no wider than what is necessary to abate the nuisance in question.

The interdict is a purely personal remedy, that is to say, an interdict is directed against the person who is named in the action. An existing owner of premises cannot, therefore, be interdicted in respect of a nuisance which has been committed by a previous owner.

In order to succeed in an action for interdict the pursuer must establish that some legal right or interest of his is being infringed. In other words, the pursuer must have title and interest to sue: *D and J Nicol* v *Dundee Harbour Trustees* (1915). An interdict is not available where the law provides for an alternative remedy: *Johnston* v *Thomson* (1877). The application for interdict must be timeous or prompt. In *Lowson's Trustees* v *Crammond* (1964) an application for an interdict to prevent the erection of buildings was refused since the buildings which were the subject-matter of the action were just about to be completed.

Simply because the subject matter of the proceedings has social utility or value does not preclude an interdict from being granted: *Webster* v *Lord Advocate* (1984).

The court has no jurisdiction to grant interdict against the Crown or against any of its officers where the result would be to grant relief against the Crown: Crown Proceedings Act 1947, ss 21(2) and 43(a). See, however, *R* v *Secretary of State for Transport, ex parte Factorame (No 2)* (1991) where the European Court of Justice held that if a national court decided that the only obstacle which precluded it from granting an interim injunction (which is the English equivalent of interdict) was a national rule of law, that rule had to be set aside.

DECLARATOR

A declarator is a judicial remedy where the court simply makes a statement of the pursuer's legal rights, for example that a particular adverse state of affairs ranks as a nuisance in law: *Webster* v *Lord Advocate*. The declarator does not order the defender to do anything. The court will only grant a declarator in relation to a matter which constitutes a live practical issue between the parties concerned in contrast to something which is purely academic or hypothetical: *Macnaughten* v *Macnaughten* (1953).

A declarator may be sought with other remedies such as interdict: *Webster* v *Lord Advocate* and *Edinburgh and District Water Trustees* v *Clippens Oil Co Ltd* (1889).

DAMAGES

The award of damages is the normal form of remedy for a delictual wrong. "Money is the universal solvent. Everything can be turned into money that is either a gain or a loss. Money is asked and damages are due for reparation of every possible suffering or injury": *Auld* v *Shairp* (1874). The purpose of the award of damages is to effect *restitutio in integrum*, that is to restore the pursuer as far as possible to the position he was in before the relevant delictual conduct took place: Stair, 1.9.2.

The law of delict in Scotland is not concerned with punishing the wrongdoer. It is about compensating the victim: *Gibson* v *Anderson* (1846). However, in relation to damages for personal injury it is unrealistic to talk of *restitutio in integrum*. Can one really be restored to one's original position in relation to a lost limb? It is more realistic, therefore, in such circumstances to describe the damages which the court awards as "compensation".

The amount of damages which the court awards bears no relationship to the degree of fault on the part of the defender.

Damage to property

Where property has been damaged the pursuer is entitled to the cost of repair of damage to the property. In relation to damages for the total loss of corporeal property the court calculates damages based on the market value of the property concerned. For example, in *Hutchison* v *Davidson* (1945) a house was burned to the ground. The Inner House held that damages should be based on the difference between market values before and after the fire which destroyed the premises. *Hutchison* concerned heritable property. However, the same principle applies to moveable property: *The Susquehanna* (1926).

The pursuer is also entitled to recover economic loss which derives from the damage in question. However, economic loss which derives from the impecuniosity of the pursuer is normally not recoverable: *Liesbosch Dredger* v *SS Edison* (1933). But the courts have never felt particularly comfortable about this decision and have proceeded to award damages to compensate loss which directly derives from the impecuniosity of the pursuer: *McIver* v *Judge* (1994).

It should be remembered here that, generally speaking, one cannot recover for pure economic loss in the law of delict: *McFarlane* v *Tayside Health Board* (2000).

Damages for personal injury

The pursuer is entitled to reparation in respect of his personal injury and any derivative economic loss. However, *no* monetary sum can really compensate the pursuer for physical injury: see, for example, *Admiralty Commissioners* v *SS Valeria* (1922).

Solatium

An award of damages for *solatium* represents compensation for the pain and suffering the pursuer has suffered as a result of the defender's conduct.

Where pain and injury will continue after the date of proof the *solatium* award will be apportioned between past and future *solatium*. In making a *solatium* award the court takes into account the gravity and extent of the relevant injury; the pursuer's awareness of any pain; the pain and suffering which has been already experienced; future pain and suffering; loss of amenity (ie enjoyment of life); and the impact on the pursuer of his awareness that his life expectancy has been diminished.

Patrimonial loss

Patrimonial loss covers all pecuniary or financial loss which is sustained by the pursuer. The court takes into account both past and future pecuniary loss. Past patrimonial loss covers losses sustained between the date of the delictual act and the date of the proof whereas future patrimonial loss relates to losses which the pursuer will suffer subsequent to the proof. The latter loss is of particular relevance in relation to severe injury. Generally speaking, the younger the pursuer is the more matters which require to be taken into account when calculating patrimonial loss such as loss of career promotion opportunities.

As far as the loss of *past* earnings is concerned, the pursuer's net income requires to be established. This is done by deducting tax, national insurance contributions and pension contributions In order to assess future loss of earnings the court must establish the net annual earnings of the pursuer as at the date of proof: *McGarrigle* v *Babcock Energy Ltd* (1996). This is known as the *multiplicand*. One then finds the *multiplier*. This is determined by taking into account the pursuer's age and probable retirement age. The multiplier is usually less than the remaining number of years which the pursuer has to work, since one must take into account uncertainties such as the possibility of redundancy, death, accidents etc. Once the multiplier and the multiplicand have been established they are simply multiplied together in order to give a lump sum. However, if the pursuer is able to work in some capacity after the accident, the court is required to establish the difference between likely future earnings which the pursuer would have earned had the pursuer not been disabled (the multiplicand) and then apply the appropriate multiplier: *Stark* v *Lothian and Borders Fire Board* (1993).

In some cases the court will not employ the multiplicand/multiplier method of calculating future patrimonial loss. For example, where the pursuer has been able to continue working, albeit on lighter work than formerly, or where there is evidence that the pursuer will be able to continue working in a lower paid job than previously: *Stevenson* v *British Coal Board* (1989).

Interest is payable on damages under the Interest on Damages (Scotland) Act 1958, as amended by the Interest on Damages (Scotland) Act 1971.

Loss of pension rights are also taken into account (*Barratt* v *Strathclyde Fire Brigade* (1984)), as are outlays and expenses. For example, damages can be recovered in respect of maintenance costs (*McMillan* v *McDowell* (1993)); reasonable medical expenses (*Lewis* v *Laird Line* (1925)); nursing costs (*McIntosh* v *NCB* (1988)). It is irrelevant if similar treatment is available on the NHS: Law Reform (Personal Injuries) Act 1948, s 2(4). Both past and future outlays require to be taken into account.

Sometimes when someone is injured that person may seek compensation:

(a) in relation to services which are rendered to him *by* his relatives as a result of such injuries; and/or

(b) services which, owing to his injuries he is no longer able to render *to* his relatives.

As far as "(a)" is concerned, s 8(1) of the Administration of Justice Act 1982 provides that where necessary services have been rendered to the injured person by a relative (as defined in s 13, as amended) then unless the relative has expressly agreed – in the knowledge that an action for damages has been raised or is in contemplation – that no payment should be made in respect of those services, the responsible person is liable to pay the injured person by way of damages such sum as represents reasonable remuneration for those services and reasonable expenses which are incurred in connection therewith. The relative has no right of action against the wrongdoer: s 8(4). Under the Law Reform (Miscellaneous Provisions) (Scotland) Act 1990 (which amends the 1982 Act), s 8(3) of the latter now permits recovery of the cost of necessary services which are rendered by a relative after the date of an award of damages. The injured party is under a duty to account to the relative for past services but not for future services.

As far as "(b)" is concerned, this head is of special importance for housewives. If the pursuer has died, the relative can claim under s 9(2) of the 1976 Act. If the pursuer is still alive, only the pursuer can claim: s 9(4).

The quantification of damages is more difficult and speculative in relation to children. The court will usually consider how the child is performing at school and his intelligence etc.

Under the Social Security (Recovery of Benefits) Act 1997 the Government can recover certain state benefits which have been paid in relation to an accident etc where the person claiming the benefits also receives compensation from a third party. This prevents the injured person from being compensated twice for the same injury. Recoupable benefits include income support, disability benefits, mobility allowance and attendance allowance.

Damages where the pursuer has died

It may sometimes happen that the pursuer, who has sustained harm which has been caused by the defender, dies before the relevant trial. Under the Damages (Scotland) Act 1976 (as amended by the Damages (Scotland) Act 1993) a claim for *solatium* up to the date of death of the injured party transmits to the executor in the same way as patrimonial loss: s 2. The death of the injured party need not have been caused by the defender.

Section 1 (as amended) of the 1976 Act allows a non-patrimonial award to be made for loss which used to be referred to as a "loss of society" award. The non-patrimonial loss award can only be claimed by the immediate family of the deceased which includes a spouse or cohabitee (including civil partner), a parent, a child or someone who has been accepted by the deceased as a child of the family. The non-patrimonial award which the immediate family can claim provides for compensation in respect of distress and anxiety endured in contemplation of the deceased before death, grief and sorrow caused by the deceased's death and loss of such non-patrimonial benefit as the immediate family member might have expected from the deceased's society and guidance if the deceased had not died.

It often happens that the deceased may have financially supported relatives prior to his death. Section 1 of the Damages (Scotland) Act 1976 allows a wider group of individuals (than those who can sue for a non-patrimonial loss award) to claim for such loss.

PRESCRIPTION AND LIMITATION

Prescription

Under s 6 of the Prescription and Limitation (Scotland) Act 1973 (PLSA) the obligation to make reparation for a delictual act is extinguished after 5 years. The relevant period runs from the date on which the delict is complete. Time begins to run when the pursuer became aware or could, with reasonable diligence, have become aware of the harm in question: s 11(3). There must be a concurrence of *damnum* and *iniuria* before the prescriptive period can commence to run. Delictual liability in relation to personal injury and death no longer prescribes: ss 6(2) and 7(2).

Some obligations are subject to what is known as long negative prescription and become prescribed only after a period of 20 years: s 7(1). An example of such long negative prescription would be an action for interdict for a nuisance which has been in existence for more than 20 years. However, an action for damages in relation to a nuisance which injures my property, and in relation to which I demand compensation from the defender, would prescribe after 5 years.

Limitation

Whereas claims for death and personal injury are imprescribable, such claims are subject to the rules on limitation. A claim for reparation in respect of death and personal injury must be brought within 3 years of the relevant injury or death: ss 17 and 18. As far as claims for personal injury are concerned, the relevant date begins to run from the date on which the injury was sustained or the act or omission ceased, whichever is the later. One takes into account the date on which either the pursuer became aware or it would have been reasonably practicable for him to become aware that his injuries are sufficiently serious to justify proceedings and that they were attributable to an act or omission of the defender. As far as a child is concerned, the relevant action must be raised within 3 years of the child attaining the age of 16: Age of Legal Capacity (Scotland) Act 1991, s 1.

Finally, the court has power to allow an action to proceed outwith the 3-year period if it deems it equitable to do so: PLSA, s 19A.

Essential Facts

- The interdict prevents an existing wrong from continuing or prevents a wrong from being done in the future.
- An interdict may be perpetual or interim.
- The pursuer must establish that some legal right or interest of his is being infringed.
- A declarator is a judicial remedy where the court simply makes a statement of the pursuer's legal rights.
- The award of damages is the normal remedy for a delictual wrong. The purpose of damages is to restore the pursuer, as far as possible, to the position he was in before the relevant delictual act took place.

- Where property has been damaged the pursuer is entitled to the cost of repair of damage to the property.
- The pursuer is also entitled to recover economic loss which derives from the damage in question.
- As far as damages for personal injury are concerned, the pursuer is entitled to reparation for injury to his person and any derivative economic loss.
- Where pain and injury will continue after the date of proof, the *solatium* award will be apportioned between past and future *solatium*.
- The court takes into account past and future pecuniary loss.
- The pursuer can recover in relation to services rendered to him by his relatives as a result of the accident and services which he is no longer able to render to his relatives.
- The obligation to make reparation for a delictual act is extinguished after 5 years. Claims for death and personal injury are subject to the rules on limitation and must be brought within 3 years of the relevant injury or death.

INDEX